EMIGRATION
AND
IMMIGRATION

Second Edition

By FRANKLIN D. SCOTT
Northwestern University

WITH THE ASSISTANCE OF
RICHARD BERINGER
California State College at Hayward

COMMITTEE ON TEACHING OF THE

AMERICAN HISTORICAL ASSOCIATION

Emigration and Immigration

By FRANKLIN D. SCOTT

Migration and History

Man's history is a story of movement, of the conquest of land from nature and from fellow man, of adaptation to new environments, of the blending of blood and the intermixture of cultures, of a constant, restless striving for "something better." At least this is the history of the peoples who have pursued progress. Non-migratory peoples have remained static—for example, the Bushmen of South Africa or Australia. Civilization may have begun when our savage ancestors found caves, built permanent campfires, and settled down. Yet by sitting still men did not find new resources or develop new ideas. The spread of ideas and people began when disaster or overcrowding forced men to move, or when they were drawn on by the lure of greener pastures and the challenge of the unknown.

Migration takes many forms. Sometimes it is the individual probing into the woods beyond the clearing, across the swamp, or over the mountain. Sometimes it is the push of armed hosts such as the invasion of the Huns into Europe, or the infiltration of the Roman Empire by the Teutonic hordes. It may be an originally peaceful but coordinated movement such as the Great Trek in South Africa. Or it may be the search for fresh grasslands for their flocks as among the tribes of ancient Asia, or the seasonal herding of their reindeer by the Lapps. It can be also the sending out of colonies to hold the frontiers of empire, or the exile of political minorities which extended Greek culture around the Mediterranean. Migration may be internal from region to region, or from country to city, or it may be a seasonal or occupational flow of people within a country or between countries. The greatest of all the chapters in the history of migration, and the one that concerns us most herein, was different

1

in numbers and extent and even in character: it was the accumulation of millions of individual and small group movements; it extended over a period of four centuries; it took some 68,000,000 people from Europe and scattered them literally over the earth; it gave birth to new nations and roused old nations from their torpor; it Europeanized the world so well that "the lesser breeds without the law" (to use the phrase of Kipling, poet of empire) have adopted Europe's methods to throw Europe back on her heels; and thus the remarkable epoch of European expansion, colonization, emigration, has come to an end.

This tremendous migratory surge began when Europe discovered the "great frontier" of America and the other sparsely peopled lands such as Australia and South Africa. It was associated with the decline of feudalism in Europe, and it has hastened the end of feudal society—for migration is a feature of a free society; bondage to the land cannot survive when man is free to move. The tempo of movement was accelerated with increasing freedom, with new developments in shipping and means of communication, and with a complex and cumulative host of factors repelling people from the Old World and attracting them to the New. But certain broad and fundamental causes underlay the entire phenomenon.

The most powerful factor impelling emigration was an extraordinary increase in population, *preceding* the ability of agriculture to feed it or of industry to give it jobs. In 1650 approximately 545,000,000 human beings lived on this planet; 300 years later the number had grown to about 2,500,000,000—more than a four-fold increase. Europe's people increased from c. 100,000,000 to 560,-000,000, and during the same period she was sending abroad *permanently* some 40,000,000. Without the safety valve of the "great frontier," would Europe have suffered the crowding and the famines and cultural slowdown of Asia? We cannot know. We do know that as the death rate declined, and before the birth rate responded to keep things in balance, emigration skimmed off a significant portion of the surplus. This not only relieved Europe's numbers, but in transoceanic fields the emigrants from Europe raised wheat to feed the people who stayed home.

The population problem went hand in hand with economic pressures—occasionally in the stark form of hunger. The potato blight of the 1840's hit western Europe hard, and it left many an Irishman with the simple choice between starvation and emigration. Fortunately the pressures of hunger and joblessness were usually less severe. More often they acted as on a young Swede, one of seven sons, who saw that the patrimony would be too small for seven new families; against his father's will he crossed the sea, and he was one of the happy ones who made a fortune. The general operation of economic causation is illustrated by the fluctuations in the stream of emigration: it was shallowest during periods of prosperity in Europe and depression in the United States, and it swelled to a flood when Europe faced hard times and America rode a crest of prosperity. But variations and contradictions arose, too, from local conditions and from individual sectors of the economy.

This phenomenon of the business cycle in relation to migration indicates also that the causes of migration were located both in the country of origin and in the country of destination. Neither the push nor the pull functioned alone. Reasons there had to be for disappointment and frustration at home, but also reasons for hope in the new country. There appears to be a correlation not only with temporary swings of the economic pendulum, but with the stages of economic development. If one takes W. W. Rostow's chart of the "Stages," he can see that for four countries at least (Germany, Sweden, Russia, and Japan) the flood tide of emigration coincided with the take-off into industrialization—in other words, the largest emigration came at just that moment when the old economic order was giving way to the new, and when there was maximum disturbance of employment. (This hypothesis calls for careful research.) Basic economic factors were also indicated by the fact that it was neither the wealthy nor the very poor who left their homelands. The wealthy had too much at stake to tear up roots; the extremely poor had neither the passage money nor the stamina nor the vision to undertake the great adventure. The vast majority of emigrants were therefore from the lower-middle economic strata, people who had a little but had an appetite for more.

Of the multitude of other causative forces, besides population and economics, the most important was probably religion. The Jews at repeated times, from the Diaspora to the return to Israel, illustrated the religious motivation. The motives of both Pilgrims and Puritans were fundamentally religious. Groups like these were exercising their rights to flee from oppression, to seek freedom. In other cases the demand was for political freedom, as with refugees from the 1848 revolutions, from Nazi Germany in the 1930's, from Communist Russia after 1917. Often migration was literally forced, as in the Greco-Turkish exchange of populations after World War I and the great refugee movements after World War II. These and other general factors, such as the desire to escape military service, appeared as causes for large numbers of emigrants, but purely personal causes were also effective.

The great migration of the nineteenth and twentieth centuries was a movement of indivduals. Each person had to make his own decision even if he came with a group. And millions came entirely alone. They were affected by the deep-seated social causes of migration, but they were more immediately driven by the circumstances of their own lives, by factors such as disappointment in love, a brush with the police, a dispute with the boss, an overbearing father, or an urge for adventure. Reasons and combinations of reasons could be numbered to infinity. The only factors universally applicable were dissatisfaction with things as they were and hope in what might be elsewhere.

Most of these millions of emigrants were young—the bulk of them in the 15 to 35 year age bracket. And most were male (85 per cent in the case of the early Austrian emigration), especially in the late nineteenth century rush as new nationalities suddenly awoke to the call of the New World. The proportion of the sexes evened out after the first or second decade when the men of the advance guard had saved enough money to send for sweethearts or families, or when demand for domestic servants provided jobs for girls. Some of them were rebels and misfits in their own countries; practically all were the unhappy, the propertyless or dispossessed, the restless and frustrated. But for the most part these same people were also the virile, the industrious, the hopeful, men with vision and drive and a love of adventure, men who could look to the future, strong young men.

As they became immigrants in a new land, some, even of the strong, were broken by the magnitude of the task or by sheer ill fortune. Others less hardy found themselves misfits and disappointed wherever they went; by migration they only exchanged one set of adversities for another. The new slums might be worse than the old, or the isolation of the frontier could be unbearable. Some suffered massacre by Indians, others died in malarial swamps, more were broken by the competitive struggle in factories and offices. Several millions returned more or less quietly to their homes, others kept moving on and on, searching and hoping until they died. The totality of disillusionments and calamites was at least a third of the immigrant flow. But these, like the casualties of an army, were sloughed off; these were not the men and women who left the lasting impact. Perhaps they should have a monument, but the successful survivors would have to build it.

The survivors of this creative movement were legion. They peopled the empty spaces of the earth. In America they pioneered the prairies or restored the farms abandoned by the westward-moving, earlier settlers. They built railroads and stoked factory furnaces, did domestic chores. They set up shops that grew into stores; they made watches, and glass, and clothes; they built bridges and buildings; they mined coal and ores. They established churches and schools and newspapers. They brought with them muscles and skills and dreams and ideas. They made farms and towns and cities, not alone but in cooperation with the heirs of earlier immigrants. Together they built. The newcomers faced tensions and misunderstandings because of differences in language and background and exacerbated by the rivalries of the struggle up from poverty. But they learned to work together, to tolerate if not to understand the differences among them. They developed new interests and new loyalties. They learned the English language and American ways. They intermarried. They grew in education and wealth. They, in all their variety of generations and national origins, became the American nation.

The three and one-half centuries of European-American migration constitute in magnitude and significance one of the greatest, if not the greatest, of all chapters in the entire annals of man's mobility. Complex and changing from period to period, this migration is worth examining in its varied facets.

The Colonial Period in North America

The voyage of Columbus opened a new era in world history, a "Boom Era" no one in the fifteenth century could have foreseen. It was to be expected that sooner or later Europeans would discover the New World of the Americas; indeed the Vikings had done it, although their exploits were not generally known by the time of Columbus' voyage. Educated men were aware that the world was round, and the idea that one might sail west to reach the East was not held by Christopher Columbus alone.

If man's geographical knowledge was so advanced that such a voyage had long seemed possible, why did he wait until 1492? The answers are complex and uncertain and can perhaps best be summed up by saying that Europe was not ready at an earlier time. But by the fifteenth century navigational, technical, and shipbuilding skills had made progress, western European states were in the process of consolidation, and it had become important to find a water route to the Far East which would by-pass Italian monopolists in the Mediterranean. This need apparently spurred the Portuguese to explore a route going south around Africa and inspired the Spaniards to look to the west. Thus the Spanish and Portuguese were to be the first to become great world explorers and, in the vast unknown, to carve out new realms for their soverigns to govern. In the Americas they found the Indians with cultures ranging from that of the hunters of the plains to the highly developed civilizations of the Aztecs and the Incas.

Whence had the Indians come? Probably they came from Asia by crossing through the far northwest where Asia and North America reach out to one another. Whether they sledded over winter's ice, or paddled in primitive boats, or walked across a now-vanished land bridge between Siberia and Alaska, we may never know. Nor do we know exactly when they came, but they had reached the valley of Mexico about 11,000 years ago, and the crossing of the Bering Strait may have been as much as 15,000 to 30,000 years ago. In all directions they diffused, in a process taking centuries, moving eastward into the plains, through the plateau of Mexico, and down beside the Andes. Some reached the extreme tip of South America, near the Straits of Magellan, where radiocarbon dating indicates arrival about 8,000 years ago.

With the coming of the Europeans, the Indians of Central and South America mixed considerably with the Hispanic conquerors. But in North America very little blending took place. Instead the Indians were gradually pushed west by the numbers and the firearms of the white man, and by his insatiable desire for land. Others of the northern Indians went west of their own volition as they got guns from white traders and used them to conquer from other tribes better hunting grounds than those they had left. Some moved into the plains, as the multiplication of the horses left by the Spaniards made it easier to gain a living by following the bison. But the tragic drama of the push westward is essentially a story of migration forced upon the Indians and, at the same time, an epic of the penetration of a continent by a new wave of immigrants who were white and had come from across the Atlantic.

In North America the shock troops and the pace setters of European occupation were the English. They settled peaceably when they could, for they sought land, not conflict. But they would not be denied; they became ruthless when it seemed necessary, and in the course of a few generations they overwhelmed the continent and made it the white man's. Yet it was more than a hundred years after Columbus that the English established their first permanent colony at Jamestown in 1607. Then the beachheads grew—at Plymouth, along the Hudson and Delaware, steadily expanding, pushing inward. Promotional companies formed, and eager settlers came—not all English. As early as 1610, for example, Italian craftsmen worked in Jamestown, and the first Negroes arrived in 1619. But why did people come?

Like later immigrants, the colonists who came to America in the 169 years before the Declaration of Independence came for a variety of reasons—religious, political, economic, and personal. A glance at the writings of Richard Hakluyt might be instructive. In 1584 he wrote *A Discourse Concerning Western Planting* in an effort to get Queen Elizabeth's support for the colonizing ventures of Sir Walter Raleigh. Among the reasons he gave for English colonization of the New World were fertility of the soil and year-round safe passage. But, more important, he felt that England suffered from over-population and that colonies would provide jobs for the sturdy beggars who filled the roads with their wandering. Hakluyt argued that the unemployed could manufacture naval stores in the forests of the New World; the colonies could provide cheap raw materials, thereby creating employment for Englishmen; demand for shipping would result in jobs for sailors; and colonies would be opportune places to locate discharged soldiers at the end of the war with Spain, thereby keeping them from swelling the ranks of the unemployed at home. Other economic advantages were said to be the avoidance of foreign ports and tariffs on goods which could now ·be gotten from colonies and the increase of English trade.

Hakluyt also used political arguments. The great enemy was Spain. To plant a colony in North America "may stay the Spanish king from flowing over all the face of that waste [vast] firmament of America." And the naval encouragement resulting from colonization would enable England "to spoil Philip's Indian navy, and to deprive him of yearly passage of his treasure to Europe, and consequently to abate the pride of Spain and of the supporter of the great anti-Christ of Rome." In other words, colonies would provide harbors for pirate ships attacking the gold convoys of the Catholic king whose riches were causing European prices to rise and who could afford, because of the windfalls from overseas, to hire a large army in Europe. How fully this argument combined economic, political, and religious justifications (and prejudices)! Though no concrete national colonization plan resulted from Hakluyt's efforts, the reasons given later when the successful colonies were established were quite similar, and the goals of government policy toward colonies were to be very much like those Hakluyt had outlined.

While some of those engaged in colonizing did so primarily out of love for adventure, and others really did not know why they were involved, it seems that the major reasons were economic. Economic motivations were primary for the unsuccessful colonies in Newfoundland and on Roanoke Island, and for the first permanent colony at Jamestown. The Jamestown colonists were so eager for profit that they neglected their crops. As John Smith wrote, "There was no talke, no hope, nor worke, but dig gold, wash gold, refine gold, load gold. . . . Never did anything more torment him [Smith], than to see all necessarie businesse neglected, to fraught such a drunken ship with so much gilded durt." Ironically this "gold" was only iron pyrite, fool's gold.

While Jamestown and the Carolinas were founded for economic reasons, religious motivations blended strongly with economic goals in the founding and settlement of the early New England colonies. Hakluyt also stated that New England could "provide a safe and sure place to receive people from all parts of the world that are forced to flee for the truth of God's word." This fit the requirements of Pilgrim, Puritan, and Quaker leaders exactly; dissenters and Catholics both used the opportunity to colonize to escape the Church of England. Even among these groups religious and economic motivations blended. The familiar story of the Pilgrims tells only the religious side, and of all religious groups they were one of the most sincere. But the majority at Plymouth was not Pilgrim, and the colony was financed by a company which sought not religious freedom, but profit. This dualism is more pronounced in the case of the Puritans. The first governor of the Massachusetts Bay Colony, John Winthrop, for instance, feared the judgment of God upon England and believed it a great service to preserve a pure remnant in the New World. But he also thought that the founding of such a colony would be wrong unless it could be an economic success, and he thought too that a colony could alleviate economic depression in England. This mixture of religious and economic motives may also be seen in the Quaker settlement of Pennsylvania and in the settlement of Maryland. In the latter Lord Baltimore, the proprietor, wanted to build up a landed estate; he further wanted to find a place where his fellow Catholics could worship freely. In Pennsylvania, William Penn sincerely sought refuge for his fellow Quakers and other Pietists, but he also wanted his quitrents paid.

Of course political reasons were also much involved in the establishment of the English colonies. The religious disabilities which Quakers and Catholics sought to avoid were a part of the political system in England, and during the Civil War and interregnum many of the colonists were refugees from political disorder. Likewise political was the desire to expand the territory and power of the kingdom.

The colony of Georgia was partly a humanitarian project, where "Many men of excellent wits and of diverse singular gifts, overthrown by suretyship, by sea, or by some folly of youth, that are not able to live in England, may there be raised again, and do their country good service." Thus James Oglethorpe led the establishment of Georgia not only to provide a buffer for the colonies against Spain, not only to tap the rich fur trade of the southern frontier, but also to provide a refuge for those imprisoned for debt and for Protestants who left the continent because of religious persecution.

If the English settled their colonies for a combination of religious, political, and economic reasons, so too did other Europeans who came to colonial America. With some, religious reasons played a predominant role. Among the most outstanding groups to flee the religious persecutions of Europe were the Huguenots. After the revocation of the Edict of Nantes in 1685 these Protestants had to flee France; they scattered widely, with one group going to South Africa and some 15,000 coming to the United States. They were not as numerous, however, as the various German Pietist groups, whose reasons for emigrating were also primarily religious. The Thirty Years' War and its horrors had helped to stimulate in Germany a more introspective religion, both in the Lutheran and Reformed Churches and in the new Pietist sects such as the Mennonites and Moravians. These religious groups often found life uncomfortable in Germany, for they had notions of church and state, of pacifism, and of oath-taking that were not welcomed by the petty German princes under whom they lived. They were attracted to the colonies in large part through the efforts of William Penn, who, while visiting the continent in 1677, had met these Pietists, whose beliefs were similar to those of the Quakers.

Political events brought other colonists. In several instances Scottish rebel prisoners were sent forcibly, notably after the Jacobite rebellions in 1715 and 1745, and many Scotch-Irish came because of the exclusion of dissenters from office by the Test Act of 1704. The religious factor produced an added impulse, for, as Presbyterians, the Scotch-Irish had difficulties with the established Church of England. And the third great factor, economic difficulty, reinforced the other two. The Scotch-Irish were descendants of those Scots who had moved to northern Ireland early in the seventeenth century. Though they became firmly established, a century later large numbers moved again, not only to America, but also to England, Germany, France, Spain, the West Indies, and even back to Scotland. The big blow against their existence in Ireland came in 1699, when the Wool Act prohibited export of Irish woolens except to England or Wales. This deprived their basic industry of important markets and became the major reason for the second move, out of Ulster to new and scattered homes. Others left later when harvests failed and rents rose, and just prior to the American Revolution the decline of the linen industry induced even more to leave. Economics affected also the Scots, who must not be confused with the Scotch-Irish. As an independent country prior to the Act of Union with England in 1707, Scotland had sent few colonists to America. But after that, in addition to the rebels mentioned above, many left because of a depressed economy and agricultural dislocation.

Hope for economic gain and political power actuated the Dutch in the founding of New Netherlands on the Hudson and the Swedes in the establishment of New Sweden on the Delaware. Both peoples and both hopes were disappointed. The Swedish-Finnish colonists were soon conquered by the Dutch (1655), but they contributed the log cabin to America and left tenacious cultural remnants along the Delaware River. The Dutch settlements were sufficiently populuous that their impress remained rather strikingly in New York long after they in turn were overwhelmed by the English (1664).

Other national groups came in varying numbers and settled throughout the colonies. In the colonial period a few besides the English settled in New England. The Huguenots, for example, sent 150 families to Massachusetts within two years after the revocation of the Edict of Nantes, and others to Maine and Rhode Island. But Indians and whites alike were inhospitable, and the settlements dispersed. The Huguenots also settled in New York and Pennsylvania, but those in the latter area are hard to trace, for they came from Alsace-Lorraine or had spent time in Germany or Holland. Thus they were soon assimilated into the German element. Others came to Virginia, but most numerous were those in South Carolina, where their major settlement was at Charleston. They assimilated easily and rapidly.

The Germans were a far more numerous body of colonists than were the French. The response to Penn's promotional efforts was great, and a steady stream of Germans continued to arrive after his death. Frictions developed between them and the English, and in 1753 Benjamin Franklin wrote Peter Collinson that he feared serious disorder, for

Those who came hither are generally the most stupid of their own nation, and as ignorance is often attended with great credulity, when knavery would mislead it, and with suspicion when honesty would set it right; and, few of the English understand the German language, and so cannot address them either from the press or pulpit, it is almost impossible to remove any prejudices they may entertain. . . . Not being used to liberty, they know not how to make modest use of it.

He concluded that the Germans should go elsewhere or they would soon outnumber the English, "and even our government will become precarious." By 1766 Franklin could report to Parliament that one-third of the Pennsylvania populace were Germans; they totalled between 110,000 and 150,000 a decade later. Their distinctive language and customs survive to this day—the "Pennsylvania Dutch" should be called *Deutsch*, for they were German and to some extent Swiss. Many went on through Pennsylvania, going to the backcountry and then south down the Cumberland Valley and into the Shenandoah. It is worth reminding ourselves, too, that an indeterminable number of the Hessians brought over to fight in the Revolution deserted and stayed as settlers in this same region.

Diligent in labor and faithful in religion, the Germans were in some contrast to the Scotch-Irish with whom they often intermingled on less than friendly terms. Though many Scotch-Irish settled in Maryland and South Carolina, their most important settlements were in Pennsylvania. Here they settled in roughly the same area as the Germans, going to the backcountry and later pushing south along the broad river valleys. These Ulstermen seemed well fitted for the hazards of frontier life, though they were thought turbulent and blasphemous in New England, and in Pennsylvania they got on so poorly with the Germans that in 1743 no more were allowed to settle in the predominantly German counties. Perhaps as many as a quarter million of these Scotch-Irish came to America in the colonial era.

Other groups came, too, in smaller numbers: Swiss, Irish, Jews, and individuals from everywhere. But the census of 1790 estimated that the English, Scots, Scotch-Irish, and Germans composed 83 per cent of the population, with the English by far the largest single group.

Cutting across nationality lines was a type of immigrant who deserves special consideration. The indentured servant might be of any nationality, and the thing that made him different was that he was not fully a free man. One of the greatest needs of the colonies was a cheap, dependable labor supply. Indentured servitude was a means of satisfying this need. The servant was usually one whose passage to the colonies was paid for him, on the condition that he work off the cost with a specified number of years of labor, usually between four and seven. Many of these people were convicts who had the not-too-difficult choice of the colonies or the gallows; some few were prisoners of war. Most were simply impoverished people who wanted to leave the homeland. They fitted into two categories. First was the indentured servant proper, who sold his services in the form of an "indenture" or contract to an agent or ship captain, who would in turn sell these indentures to a merchant or planter in the colonies. The second type was the redemptioner, or man who had expected to pay his own passage; when his funds ran short he was given space aboard ship on condition that he be indentured for a term long enough to repay his passage.

Some colonies were so short of population that to stimulate immigration a grant of land, known as a headright, was given for each colonist brought over. A free man received this himself. An indentured servant, however, represented a grant of land for the individual who paid his way, creating an additional source of profit. The conditions of the trade were deplorable. In some cases jails were emptied, or parishes took the opportunity to lower their burden of poor relief. To fill the "cargo," agents travelled through the countryside, telling exaggerated stories of the New World and stimulating the "America fever." These "newlanders," as they were called, did not feel called upon to adhere closely to the truth, and kidnapping was not infrequently used to fill the ship when volunteers were few.

The Atlantic crossing in those days was always a hazard, and the conditions of the servant trade made it worse. Overcrowded ships, poor food and water, and poor ventilation caused great numbers to die of disease, and the perils of shipwreck and capture by enemies added to the toll. One ship which took 24 weeks to get to the West Indies in 1751 lost almost all her passengers, and another ship 10 years earlier lost 46 of 106 passengers by starvation—6 of the dead were eaten by those who survived. One man described his voyage thus: "we had enough in the day to behold the miserable sight of botches, pox, and others devoured with lice till they were almost at death's dore [sic]. In the night fearful cries and groning

[sic] of sick and distracted persons, which could not rest, but lay tumbling over the rest, and distracting the whole company, which added much to our trouble."

One authority estimated that, except for the Puritan migrations of the 1630's, between one-half and two-thirds of the colonial white immigrants to America were indentured servants, redemptioners, and convicts. The trade declined after the Revolution and was for all practical purposes finished by 1815. The indenture system had one great disadvantage: just when a servant was fully trained and experienced, his term of service was likely to expire. The remedy was to find a labor supply which would serve for an indefinite period, and to fill this need the system of slavery was gradually introduced.

The first Negroes brought to England's American colonies came on a Dutch ship in 1619. Contrary to popular belief, these were not slaves in the usual sense of the term; in fact, the term "slave" had no legal meaning and was applied loosely to white as well as Negro servants. Until the 1660's, therefore, Negroes were treated much like white indentured servants. Some eventually were freed and themselves became owners of men. But the Negro's condition steadily worsened, and after 1700 the slave system was firmly established. The slave trade was even more lucrative than that in indentured servants, for slaves met a need for labor which the whites could not fill. Toward the end of the eighteenth century a ship carrying 250 slaves could earn £7,000 on one voyage. One hundred per cent profits per voyage were not unknown. Even more than the servant trade, the slave trade was cruel. Each of the slave-trading powers established trading stations along the West African coast. Contact was established with the chiefs or "kings" of some tribes, and permission was obtained to trade in a chief's particular area. Here textiles, metal goods, beads, arms, spirits, and foodstuffs were traded for slaves. The slaves were brought by the coastal tribes in coffles, or chained gangs, from as much as a thousand miles away, over tortuous paths. The trade had an aura of death, for, of those who reached the ship, many perished packed or chained so closely together that they could hardly move. Disease ran rampant. Many died of exhaustion on the way, and more died trying to escape or committed suicide by jumping overboard. Even for those who survived this dreaded "middle passage" the specter of death remained, since many died within the first year in the new environment.

It is difficult to determine the number of slaves who actually reached American shores, and of course they were sent not only to English colonies but to those of the French, Portuguese, Spanish, and Dutch, as well. The total number taken from Africa "ran far into the millions." According to the census of 1790, when a white population of 3,000,000 was recorded, some 750,000 Negroes lived in the United States, most in the South where they were in great demand in plantation agriculture and in all types of manual labor. Whereas there were 67,000 Negroes (40,000 of them slaves) in the North in that year, 690,000 (657,000 slaves) lived in the South. By constitutional provision (Article I, Section 9), no restriction of the slave trade could take effect before 1808, but in that year slave importation was prohibited. Two years later the census showed a population of 1,378,000 Negroes and 6,000,000 whites. An illicit foreign slave trade continued up to the eve of the Civil War, but there is no reliable estimate of the numbers imported illegally.

By the end of the Revolutionary War the pattern of the peopling of America was established. The westward movement, which began as soon as the settlements at Plymouth and Jamestown sent offshoots into the interior, gained increasing momentum until the end of the nineteenth century. Germans, English, and Scotch-Irish continued to be mainstays of the trans-Atlantic immigration, augmented by other northern and western Europeans such as the Irish and the Scandinavians. A fairly clear pattern had also emerged for the reasons that impelled people to leave the land of their ancestors and seek a new fortune across the ocean. At the same time, heralded by warnings of men like Franklin, there appeared the forerunners of those who would close the door to this New World. Perhaps nothing could better indicate that, even so early, the previous generation of immigrants thought their new country was coming of age.

To a surprising extent the new society had established itself. Offshoots of Europe, and especially of England, had been effectively transplanted, had taken root and grown. For the emigrants from Europe had not gone forth to discard their heritage. They wanted to take Europe with them but to improve upon it. Their new community might be called "Europe Revised." The emphasis in the revision was overwhelmingly English, for the English not only came early and in continuing great numbers, but they did little fraternizing with the Indians and insisted on the maintenance of their basic culture. New England was appropriately named, for it was exactly that, whereas New Spain, e.g., was comparatively much less Spanish. A striking feature of United States history is the stubborn and lasting persistence of the English impress, not exclusive but guiding, even after other nationalities were added to the scene. The English language became a language of all. The fundamental political and social structure, even the basic ideals of the new society, were well set during the founding period and to a considerable extent were codified in the Constitution and maintained in the almost universal use of common law. To a large degree it was precisely those modified Anglo-Saxon institutions and ideals, created by the first wave of immigrants, that attracted later immigrants to American shores.

Beginnings of the Big Surge, 1783-1865

The period between the American Revolution and the end of the War of 1812 showed a slackening of immigration. War and revolution disturbed both America and Europe, and travel was unsafe. But when the world settled down to peace after 1815 the new influx of immigrants began. While estimates are that 120,000 newcomers arrived in the 20 years between 1790 and 1810, almost that many arrived in the next decade, and the 1820's brought another 150,000. Of course, these figures cannot be taken too literally, for official immigration statistics were not kept until 1820, and even these were woefully inadequate. A precise accounting is impossible. We know, for instance, of Norwegian immigration which was never recorded: at least 53 immigrants arrived in 1825, though official American figures show only 4 for Norway and Sweden together, and at least 167 came in 1836, though American records show but 57 from Norway-Sweden. Furthermore, it was not until 1850 that arrivals at Pacific Coast ports were counted, and not until the twentieth century that immigrants coming via Canada were included accurately. Even so, American and European records together furnish a guide to the relative importance of immigration of the different nationalities and the relative increase or decrease of immigration over a long period of time. While the 150,000 arrivals in the 1820's seemed large, this was but preliminary, for by 1846 this figure was being exceeded in one year alone, and 400,000 came in 1854. In 1870 about one-eighth of the population of the United States was foreign born.

By and large this great mass came from the nations of northern and western Europe: Great Britain, Ireland, Germany, and, in increasing numbers, Scandinavia. Significant numbers also came from Canada, Mexico, and other Western Hemisphere countries, but we do not know how many of these people were native to an American country. This is important since, as already indicated, large numbers of European immigrants came to the United States by way of Canada.

Just as the countries of origin of these "old" immigrants were varied, so were their occupations. There was always a substantial number of farmers, and, as the period progressed, great numbers of laborers arrived. The largest single group reported no occupation. Comparatively few professional men came. Not only were professional people a smaller proportion of the homeland population, but they were usually economically better off and therefore were less likely to strike out anew.

The reasons these emigrants of the early nineteenth century made the big move from their homes, to try to begin again in this new land, were as varied as the countries from which they came. One reason for the big spurt of immigration after 1815 was the release of the dam erected by the Napoleonic Wars, but that was a temporary thing. More important were questions of religion. Among the first Norwegians to arrive were Quakers and Haugeans (a dissenting group within the state church). Resentment against an established church was an important motivation for many immigrants. In Sweden various dissenting groups rejected the rationalism of the Lutheran Church, and to escape resulting persecution many of them came to the United States, where they built settlements such as that at Bishop Hill, near Galesburg, Illinois. American missionaries in Sweden also encouraged immigration, and newly converted Baptists, Methodists, and Mormons left Sweden as a result. Many Dutch immigrants were seceders from the Reformed Church who resented petty annoyances placed upon them, and some "Old Lutheran" Prussians came in the 1830's, partly because they would not conform to the United Evangelical Church. Other Germans who had religious motivation for leaving were the Jews, banned in some states, restricted in others. With the Irish the problem was somewhat different, for the Catholic Irish were not a minority group within their nation. Perhaps this made their persecutions even more difficult to bear. The alien landowners were Church of England men, and Catholic Irishmen had to pay tithes and later a special rent to maintain the church of their hated landlords. Even when high office was finally opened to Roman Catholics in 1829, voting qualifications were raised, disfranchising many of them.

Thus political antagonisms and complications accompanied and aggravated religious difficulties. The Irish were above all bitter against English political domination and felt that because of this they had no chance to improve their lot at home. Throughout much of Europe the common man resented the domination of the upper classes, the clergy, and the bureaucracy. In Norway a leader of the small rural freeholders, who had been in parliament, was later imprisoned for sacrilege and revolutionary activity and finally emigrated to America, whence he wrote: "Now for the first time I am able to breath freely. . . . No one is persecuted here because of his religious faith." After the revolutionary disturbances of 1830 in Europe, a number of disappointed participants emigrated. The repressive aftermath of the Revolution of 1848 sent more, particularly from Germany. Although, as Marcus Lee Hansen has shown, this protest emigration was much exaggerated, it nevertheless brought to the United States some distinguished men, such as Carl Schurz, who played an important role in American politics.

More important for most than either religion or politics was the economic problem. The poverty of the old country as compared with the often overestimated riches of America turned sober farmers and artisans to thoughts of emigration. Thus both the push of conditions at home and the pull of conditions in America served as powerful stimuli. No matter how much the prospective immigrant may have loved his country, sometimes economic conditions became so intolerable that he felt forced to leave.

Farewell, Norway, and God bless thee.
  Stern and severe wert thou always,
But as a mother I honor thee,
  Even though thou skimped my bread.
All things vanish. Grief and care
  Sink down upon the heart;
Still the memory of these refreshes the soul
  Like the deep sleep of a child.

Again the Norwegian experience is illustrative. A series of bad harvests in the late 1830's created agricultural stagnation. This was intensified by the minute division of land, for as the population increased rapidly so did the number of farms. From 80,000 farms in 1802, the number rose to 135,000 by 1860. When the farm became too small to provide a living, the farmer had to seek other work, but this was not always to be found. Then the only alternatives were mortgages or poor relief. When crops failed starvation was a real danger. By the middle 'forties, two-thirds of the farms were mortgaged, and interest plus official fees could equal as much as 16 per cent of the loan. Even if the rural freeholder was himself able to get along, he often moved for the sake of his family. As one writer in the 1860's put it,

A man with one thousand dollars and five children reasons as follows: one thousand dollars divided among five children amounts to little or nothing here in this country. But if I go to America, where there is plenty of fertile land to be had for next to nothing, my little capital, combined with the industry of myself and my children, is sufficient to furnish all of us an independent and satisfactory position.

Economic depression often struck many parts of Europe. In the Netherlands in 1846 wages were low, and food taxes alone took about 14 per cent of the total annual wage. By 1850 some 27 per cent of the population needed public support. As the industrial revolution put more and more British weavers out of work in the 1820's, they too picked up to travel to America before their savings were exhausted. Growing industrialization caused trouble also in Wales. With the increasing world demand for coal and iron, land was withdrawn from agricultural production and the valleys were transformed. Fearing the fate of the landless, the farmers tried to continue farming by cultivating a few acres to supplement their wages from mining. The result was that the farmer-miner suffered whenever depression hit either agriculture or industry. The only way out for many was emigration.

Germany likewise suffered from economic dislocation. Though the revolutionary "Forty-eighters" were significant for their quality, they were unimportant in quantity; most emigrants left for primary economic reasons. For instance, the farmers of southwestern Germany were principally small holders who had mortgaged their farms to secure capital for modernization. Although emancipated from feudal obligations, when they were hit by the crop failures of the 1840's, they could not make their cash payments. Mortgages were foreclosed and farm families moved to America to recoup their fortunes. They were often joined by wealthier farmers who had no confidence in the future of German agriculture and by paupers sent out by officials who found ship fares less expensive than poor relief.

The most spectacular event which pushed the emigrant from his homeland was the potato famine. Contrary to popular belief, it did not strike only in Ireland. In the Netherlands, for instance, approximately 80 per cent of the potato lands were infected with the blight in 1845, and conditions were still bad in 1846 and 1847. To a modern American, who has plenty of beef and pork, wheat and rice, it may seem odd that the failure of a potato crop could cause much distress. Today it would not. But in the nineteenth century the potato was the basic food for the poor man of western Europe. It was nutritious, inexpensive, filling, and was often the chief article in the peasants' diet. Although potato blight had been known in the past, in the 1840's it was more serious because it was more widespread and because more people relied upon the potato. In 1845 Ireland suffered the blight not only of potatoes in the ground, but of those already harvested as well. In 1846 the blight struck again, and in Ireland it seemed like the end of the world. Since all Europe was hit, there was no aid close at hand. One source of aid was grain from America, which began to arrive in Ireland early in 1847. The grain ships brought food not only for the body but for the mind as well. Thoughts inevitably turned to a land where there was no famine and food was always available. And American grain ships in Irish harbors could supply cheap transportation for people going westward.

These forces of push, whether religious, political, or economic, seldom acted alone. More often the full motivation was a combination of these causes, plus factors of pull as well. For no matter how serious conditions might be at home, a man would not leave unless he had heard of a more promising place elsewhere and had the means to get there. It is to these latter affairs that we must now direct our attention.

Contemporary Norwegians often blamed "America fever" for the outpouring of emigrants, and an observer in Ireland reported "that those feelings and motives [regarding America] have taken a deep root, and are very widely spread." And indeed the "America fever" spread like a contagion, skipping one area and infecting the next. One town might be decimated by the emigrant outflow, and the next hardly touched. More interesting than the fever, however, is what caused it. How, for instance, did the unhappy peasant learn about America? A major agent in this education was the "America letter": a letter written by an immigrant in America to his family or friends in the old country. What a picture these letters painted! "And I can tell you that here we do not live frugally but here one has eggs and egg pancake and canned fish and fresh fish and fruits of all kinds, so it is different from you who have to sit and hold herring bones." Thus wrote one Swedish immigrant. A Norwegian in the Middle West proudly exclaimed,

Hardly a day passes without my reflecting on how richly God blesses this country every year; and then my heart is moved to pity when my thoughts go back to Norway and I recall the poor people in cities and in the country who had to beg for the bare necessities of life with tears in their eyes. How happy the poor and the landless would consider themselves if they were here, especially those who are honest in purpose and cheerful.

These letters reached not only the relatives at home. They could influence a whole village. In some instances they were read from the pulpit on Sunday mornings or published in the local newspaper. The arrival of a letter from America could be a community affair. The schoolmaster might be drafted to read it if the family was illiterate, and often copies were made to send to other villages. Families would gather around in tense expectancy: what was the news? Was there a ticket to America, and for whom?

Of course not all letters were favorable, and those that were not would often be widely publicized by those who opposed emigration. Hard times came to America, too, and then the word would get back to the old country and the current of travelers would slow.

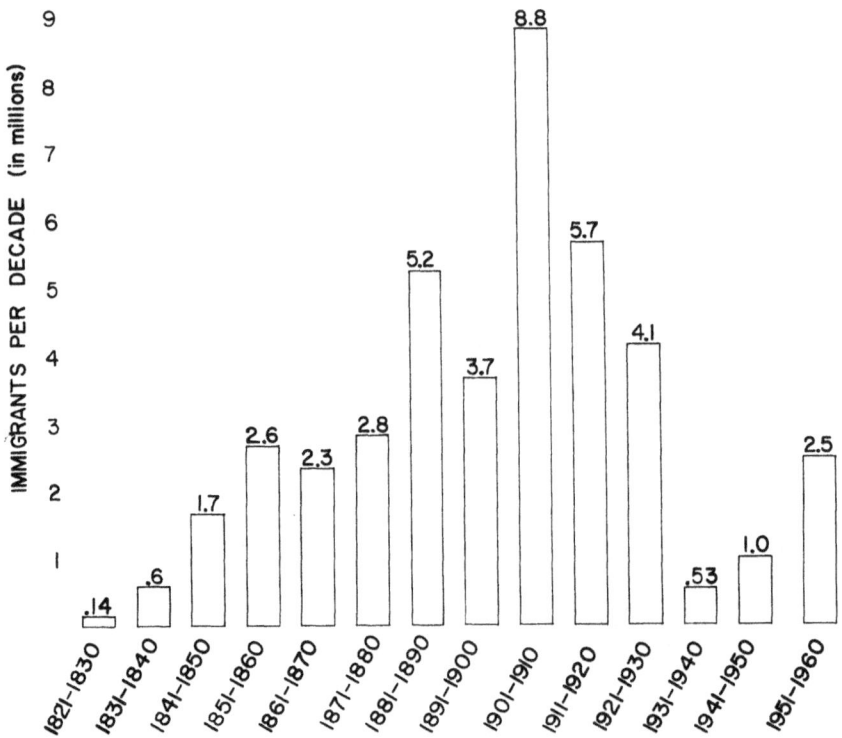

RECORDED UNITED STATES IMMIGRATION 1821–1960—TOTAL: 41.6 MILLION

One disillusioned immigrant wrote back, "only about a third part of these [America] letters is true. People only write down accounts of the good, although they themselves have had no experience of it." He went on to complain about disease, summer heat, snakes, taxes, "detestable" Mormons, and low wages.

Often just as important as the letters themselves was the money enclosed, for this served several purposes. It was tangible evidence of American wealth; it could be used to pay debts or to buy a cow; or, and this was frequent, it could be used to finance the emigration of other members of the family. For the latter purpose prepaid tickets were often sent instead of money. As early as 1848 about 40 per cent of the total Irish remittances were in the form of prepaid passages.

Also important was the myriad of guidebooks and travel accounts circulated in the homeland. These varied widely in truth and utility, but they served as publicity. The travel diary of Fredrika Bremer, a Swedish novelist who visited America in the 1850's, went through six Swedish editions and was translated into Danish and English. The outstanding advertisement of America's riches, however, was a human one, the returnee. Of course many returned who had failed, and their stories, too, would be heard. But the failure would not brag of his poor fortune the way the success bragged of his good fortune. The clothes the visitor wore, decorated perhaps with a gold watch chain, his money, and the mere fact that he could afford the trip were eloquent testimonials. Nor was the returned immigrant likely to be very reticent. One talked so much he was characterized as not "a blow but a constant blast."

Some returned immigrants had special reasons for dressing so well and bragging so loudly. These were agents (sometimes secretly) of shipping lines, railroads, construction companies, or land companies, who would get a commission for everyone they managed to recruit. Artificial enthusiasm was induced also by broadsides, which did not always conform strictly to the truth but were printed in the native language and distributed widely. Special offices were established to encourage emigration. In 1846 the agent of some Virginia land speculators established an office in Liverpool and published a pamphlet urging the parishes to send their unemployed to America. In Wisconsin, the first state Commissioner of Immigration was appointed in 1852, and agents were sent to Europe to solicit immigrants. Especially notable was the work of American railroads. Immigrants were often signed up at New York for construction work, but more important was the recruiting done in Europe to get settlers for railroad lands. The first railroad to encourage immigration was the Illinois Central which in 1854 sent its agent, an educated Swedish immigrant, to Norway and Sweden. Propaganda pamphlets were published, and in the 1860's a vigorous program was directed toward Germans, Scandinavians, and the British. Other railroads followed suit. Some private persons, too, paid their way to America by persuading others to go with them and then getting their own passage as a commission on the tickets of their friends.

Once he had decided, or been persuaded, to leave, the prospective emigrant needed passage. Occasionally groups of emigrants would go from one agent to another, bargaining with their volume of business to get lower rates. Agents got on to this early. In one case two "Yankees" (returned immigrants) demanded free transportation from Göteborg, Sweden, to Minneapolis, Minnesota, and cheap passage for the twenty-two emigrants they shepherded, on the grounds that a rival line had offered as much. The put-upon agent agreed, without letting on that the free passage would last only as far as England! Swindling and counter-swindling were rife. After 1815, the North American timber and staple trade (tobacco, cotton, etc.) engaged many ships to Europe. These ships had empty space on their return voyages, since their cargo of manufactured goods took up less room than had the raw materials. Thus the immigrant could fill space otherwise unused. Cost then was cheap, since anything received accrued to the advantage of the shipping company, and keen competition drove prices down. The Liverpool-New York steerage ticket in 1816 cost twelve pounds; in 1846 it was approximately one-fourth of that amount.

The voyage itself, little safer than in the colonial era, was not without great danger. Despite attempts of governments to regulate ship capacity, the steerage passengers were usually confined below decks with woefully inadequate space, ventilation, or sanitary facilities. A passenger was expected to furnish his own provisions, and if these ran out he had to buy from the ship's stores, usually at extravagant prices. These problems were accented by the length of the voyage, for against storms and adverse winds the sailing ships of this era might take as long as four months to cross the Atlantic. Sometimes the trip took as little as twenty-five days, but even this was a long time to spend in cramped, stuffy quarters. Although there sometimes was merriment in singing, dancing, and deck activity, frequently the passengers were too ill or the weather too rough to allow any recreation.

Disease was a serious problem. During bad weather proper food could not be prepared, and toward the end of the voyage food was often spoiled and water was brackish. Hence some vessels lost a large number of passengers due to the increasing density of the human cargoes. In 1847 one ship with 440 passengers suffered 108 deaths and arrived at quarantine with another 150 sick. The same year another ship lost 107 of 475 steerage passengers, and a third vessel had 98 dead and 112 sick of its original 399 passengers; because of disease, 84 ships were detained at Grosse Isle below

Quebec, where sickness and poor shelter killed 10,000 Irish immigrants. Shipwreck and, in a day of wooden ships, fire were constant dangers. Such problems did not cease upon arrival at an ocean port, for many immigrants immediately went west via the Erie Canal and the Great Lakes and here again faced the perils of the deep. For instance, in 1847 the propeller ship *Phoenix* burned in Lake Michigan off Sheboygan, Wisconsin, with a loss of 200 lives, mostly Dutch immigrants.

Once the voyage was over, dangers continued. As soon as the ship docked, swarms of runners pounced upon the hapless traveler and tried to lead him to boarding houses and saloons. This situation was somewhat improved by the establishment of regular receiving stations, such as Castle Garden in New York, in 1855. The experiences of the crossing were thus similar for all immigrant groups. But once on the American shore, their paths diverged.

The Irish stayed mainly in the eastern seaboard cities from Pennsylvania and New Jersey north to Massachusetts. The Dutch went to the farming regions of Michigan, Iowa, and Wisconsin, and the Scandinavians settled in Wisconsin, Minnesota, and the northern plains states. The Germans settled extensively in the Middle West, but distributed themselves widely, including important centers in the East and in Texas. The British settled in the industrial Northeast and in mining areas, but language factors probably allowed them to spread more easily throughout the land. Few settled in the South. This was seldom because of antipathy to slavery but because the southern economy did not offer workers or settlers opportunities like those available in the North.

The occupations these people followed were often like those of the homeland; the most notable exception came with the Irish, who were usually of rural origin yet seldom settled on the land. This was partly due to lack of needed capital to buy land and equipment and the parallel need to obtain employment quickly, which was, of course, more easily available in the cities. It was also attributable to the tragic memories of their native agricultural experience, their dislike of the isolation of American farm life, and the absence of priests in rural areas. Thus the Irish generally became urban laborers, firemen, and, to the glory of American folklore, policemen. The Dutch, on the contrary, settled mostly in farming areas, although many did run small shops or work in local factories. The German experience was similar, because many of them became farmers or worked in agricultural industry, but they also made important contributions in technical industries. The British likewise went into industry in significant numbers, while the Scandinavians were mostly farmers in the period before the Civil War.

This second epoch in American immigration brought an increasing diversity of people and spread them far beyond the Appalachians. The movement into the Middle West and the rapid development of California and other parts of the Far West were characterized both by new immigration straight from Europe and by a westward surging of resident Americans from New England and the Middle Atlantic regions. This westward movement represented unplanned but highly effective cooperation among settlers from the East and migrants from across the ocean. Some sought Utopia; all sought status and self-respect. Because of the newness of all and their varied backgrounds, they accepted the institutions already established. Anglo-American patterns served as the framework for the expanding society.

Mass Migration, 1865–1914

The migratory stream from Europe to America both expanded and changed toward the end of the nineteenth century. Earlier immigration had come largely from northern and western Europe, and in the 1880's this movement reached its height. This was the great decade for the Germans and the Scandinavians. In the 1890's fewer of these peoples migrated, largely because industry was developing in their homelands and the demand for labor was rising. The outflow from Europe as a whole, however, increased, for as the northern groups declined in numbers the southern increased—until early in the twentieth century the migration of Italians, Greeks, Poles, Russians, Austro-Hungarians, and others from southern and eastern Europe became a flood. The Italians exemplified the shift: 12,000 came in 1880, but by the peak year 1907 their number was 282,000, which was 22 per cent of the total.

In the period before the Civil War the banner year was 1854, with 427,000 newcomers. Between the Civil War and 1900 the peak was reached in 1882 with 800,000, northerners still predominating.

But in the first years of the twentieth century the annual influx passed the million mark six times, and in 1907 the figure rose to 1,285,000. The significance of these vast numbers for the population as a whole can be seen from the fact that by 1930 there were 14,000,000 foreign born in the United States. If the first American generation be included, the foreign stock of the United States (foreign or of mixed parentage) was almost 24 per cent of the total white population in 1920.

Small wonder that people in both Europe and America became alarmed at this spectacular transfer of population. Investigating commissions were set up and voluminous reports were issued in Italy, Sweden, and the United States. In Sweden a "Society against Emigration" attracted wide support from both employers and patriots who saw the young strength of the land disappearing. In the United States fear was expressed that industry could not continue to employ the burgeoning numbers of strangers, that they could not be assimilated into the society, and that if they were absorbed they would change the character of the nation.

The "new immigrants" who predominated in the statistics after the 1890's came for the same reasons as had their predecessors, but the people were indeed different. They differed in religious complexion, for they were mostly Greek Orthodox or Roman Catholic, entering a society that was basically Protestant; a large segment were Jews. They came from southern and eastern Europe, and they spoke a different variety of languages. Because they were generally poorer and less well educated than those who had come before, proponents of restriction advocated a literacy test. Many newcomers were frankly "birds of passage," seeking in the United States small but quick fortunes that would enable them to return home and live in ease. Fewer than before meant to settle on the land, and there was little cheap land available.

Powerful forces impelled this urgent exodus from Europe. The familiar imponderables—wanderlust, adventuresomeness, family problems—played their part. Basic religious, political, and economic discontent had major roles, and an exaggerated "myth of America" inspired hope in the hopeless. Underlying all was a very real "population explosion." Only Ireland had a net population loss during the epoch of emigration. The other countries had been increasing steadily before emigration got well started, and they kept on increasing while millions departed. Emigration only partly relieved the pressure, but it did provide an alternative for those who were disgruntled but vigorous, who were poor but not destitute, who could not find work but who could dream of a better life overseas.

Reasons for the fateful decision to emigrate had, by the late nineteenth century, somewhat changed. Religion was less often a vital factor, for Europe had become more tolerant (or indifferent). Religio-racial discrimination against the Jews, however, continued in several countries, especially in Russian Poland. In revenge for the Nihilist assassination of Alexander II, pogroms were instigated in 1881, and other massacres took place in 1882, 1903, and 1906. It is not surprising, then, that the large majority of Jewish immigrants during this period came from Russia. Others who emigrated for political and religious reasons were the Russo-German Mennonites. They had settled in the Volga and Black Sea regions in the eighteenth century when Catherine the Great had offered them free worship, extensive autonomy, and exemption from military service. When these privileges were withdrawn in 1870 the Mennonites emigrated.

Political motivations were also active. Poles resented the forcible Germanization and Russification carried out by the occupying powers in the last quarter of the nineteenth century, and after the revolutionary outbreaks of 1905 some of the participants escaped to America. Internal conditions in Poland at this time were pictured in a letter which one Pole wrote to his brother in America in November, 1906:

> About 70,000 people are tortured in prisons, hundreds have been shot and hanged. The spring . . . will probably put more innocent victims to the sword than the present winter, for the blood that is shed, the fire of cities and villages, do not subdue the people but rather kindle hatred against their persecutors and oppressors. . . . Now everything is dear, from salt and matches up to the coat on your shoulders and the wagon of firewood at the market; cheap is only the life of the poor man, because it is taken away without question, without witnesses, without court.

Political and social discontent was also an important factor in Scandinavia in this period, as it had been earlier, and in the Turkish Empire, from which both Syrians and Armenians fled.

Increasingly important was the effect of economic change. Both the threat and the promise of America were embodied in the tremendous production of wheat from the western prairies, which yielded bread but depressed prices for the small European farmer. In Italy agricultural difficulties played a major role, since most Italian emigrants were from the agricultural classes. Some redistribution of church lands benefitted only the rich, for down payments were required on all purchases. Practice of equal inheritance simultaneously caused excessive fragmentation of the smaller plots. Agricultural methods were primitive, and this brought low production and hence low income. The lack of farm animals meant a shortage of manure for fertilizer; and since a crop was needed every year, land could not be left fallow. Two "last straws" were the end of the American citrus market, due to the development of California and Florida orchards, and the French imposition of high tariffs on wine; thus two Italian export crops were hard hit.

Polish peasants had a somewhat similar experience. In 1882 peasants held an average of about seven acres. By 1896 the average was less than six. The lack of factories made it difficult to get extra work to supplement income or to balance the seasonal nature of farming. A surprising problem was added in Poland, where in some areas there were 200 church holidays a year—which left a work year of only about five months. The result of these conditions, in Poland as elsewhere, was emigration. The major cause of Greek emigration was also economic. Again, a people was plagued by backward agricultural methods, ill-requiting soil, too many religious holidays, and lagging industry. One specific economic blow was the decline of the currant market. When French vineyards were destroyed by phylloxera in the 1870's, the Greeks let silk culture decline, cut down their olive trees to make room, and turned to profitable grape growing. But as the French vines recovered at the end of the century, the bottom fell out of the market, and there were no more olive orchards to take up the economic slack. In Austria-Hungary, too, a major factor of discontent was the excessive division of land, which had proceeded rapidly since the peasant was given the right to divide his land in the 1860's. This created a landless laboring class, since there were few factories to absorb this labor. Agricultural decline in Germany and Scandinavia had also created a surplus rural labor supply, but in these countries the process of industrialization began early in the twentieth century to absorb more of the excess labor. Not only were Poland, Italy, Greece, and Austria affected by the collapse of the old agrarian order. So were Portugal, Rumania, Bulgaria, and Finland, and from these countries, too, large numbers left for America.

But just as in earlier periods, before the discontented could leave they had to know of some place to go. Of course, not all went to the United States, but the great majority did. A guiding influence again was the America letter. These America letters were like thousands of little magnets for Greeks, Portuguese, Italians, Poles, and Russians. The Polish letters, for instance, show the gradual reorientation of the immigrant in a new environment, and the constant requests for money made by the people in the old country show that the milk and honey legend which the immigrants themselves created was thoroughly accepted. One girl, working as a servant in Brooklyn, wrote her parents,

> And now I am on duty and I do well, I have fine food, only I must work from 6 o'clock in the morning to 10 o'clock at night and I have $13 a month. And now, dear parents, I implore you don't grieve about me, thinking that I am without money. . . . As it is I have spent more than 50 roubles on myself for the coming winter. . . . I have brothers and sisters and I intend to help them all to come to America.

From such letters simple peasants exaggerated the riches of the immigrants. Frequently letters back to America asked for money or steamship tickets, which, when received, evoked new requests. One letter began, "I thank you first for having sent the money," went on to explain how the writer had bought land, and ended, "send me about 100 roubles. . . . If 100 is too much for you, send at least 50." Not all letters from the West were favorable. One woman wrote back to her sister,

> My dear, in America it is no better than in our country: whoever does well, he does, and whoever does poorly, suffers misery everywhere. . . . Many people in our country think that in America everybody has much pleasure. No, it is just as in our country, and the churches are like ours, and in general everything is alike.

Immigration was also stimulated by growing organized promotion. Agents of shipping lines, railroads, and western states themselves played an important role. Ticket agencies were spread throughout Europe where colored posters gave details of the sailings, and labor bureaus were occasionally established by steamship companies. American railroads expanded their programs. For instance, in 1870 the Burlington and Missouri Railroad appointed an agent for the British Isles, who distributed thousands of handbills, circulars, and maps, and talked with influential people. This and similar work was effective, for in 1873 there were 342 Europeans settled on company lands in Nebraska, including 31 from Bohemia, 37 from Russia, 46 from Scandinavia, 113 from Germany, and 93 from Britain. Nor were state efforts unimportant. Eager developers expanded state immigration programs after the Civil War and cooperated with the railroads—the Burlington and Missouri Railroad agent mentioned above was also the agent of the Iowa State Board of Immigration!

The immigrant from the post-Civil War period, once he had decided to come, had an easier time of it than had his predecessor of the early nineteenth century. Conditions in European ports were better than they had been, the purchase of a ticket was less open to fraud, and most important was the coming of the steamship. Though the steamship had been developed before the Civil War, in 1856 96 per cent of the immigrants arriving at New York still came by sail. By 1873, however, an even greater proportion came by steam. Then a voyage could be made in about ten days instead of weeks or even months, and by 1898 the crossing from Queenstown to New York took five and one-half days. The steerage might still be cramped and dirty, but ten days in such quarters would not be so likely to cause disease and suffering as would thirty days. Food and water could now be kept fresh during the entire voyage, and resistance to disease could be maintained; the mortality rate for steerage passengers declined significantly. Other improvements came as dishonest and greedy captains, who had owned their own sailing ships, were replaced by officers selected by and working for large shipping companies. Yet steerage conditions were still deplorable, and the cramped quarters, loathsome odors, immorality, lack of privacy, and shortage of sanitary facilities, reported by a 1911 investigation, seem to show that in these respects there was little improvement over the era of sail.

The competition for the immigrant trade developed a keen rivalry among steamship companies of different nations. For east European emigrants the Germans used control stations along the Russo-German border to carry out both medical inspection and "ticket inspection": those who arrived at these points were often delayed or turned back unless they would travel on the ships of the Hamburg-America or North German Lloyd Lines. This hurt the British, for earlier emigrants had sailed across the North Sea to England, then transshipped by a British line for the Atlantic crossing. The British therefore retaliated against the German restrictions by extending their routes to Baltic and Mediterranean ports, enabling Austro-Hungarian and Russian immigrants to embark without passing the German border. The Red Star, Anchor, and Hamburg-America Lines also set up more than 6,500 ticket agencies in the United States for use of immigrants who wished to purchase prepaid tickets for relatives or friends.

Upon arrival in the United States the immigrant was met by conditions often strange and frightening. The officials in starched shirts at Castle Garden or Ellis Island in New York did not seem to understand the peasants from foreign lands. And the peasants, with the narrow outlook of their old life, suspected officials and distrusted interpreters. Probing questions about morals, politics, and previous conduct were looked upon as designed to trick those who knew no better. Even after passing quarantine and official inspection, many problems remained. Of the old immigrants many spoke English, and the British as well as the Germans and the Scandinavians often had family or friends well established in the new land. But how was an eastern European peasant expected to cope with problems of language, baggage, temporary lodging, and the purchasing of tickets? Many a native American today has a difficult time with these problems when he travels!

Of course there were always some co-nationals who were eager to help, who greeted newcomers in their native language, snatched up their baggage and, having won confidence, proceeded to fleece their victims unmercifully. Many who had hoped to go west no longer had the funds and were stranded in the port city. One story has it that a nice young man in New York helped an immigrant family bound for Kansas City by taking their money, buying their tickets, and putting them on the train, only in this case the train was the Third Avenue Elevated! Nor did these "runners" operate only in port cities. At big inland cities like Chicago they again hovered about, offering advice on baggage and railroad tickets. Other difficulties were due not so much to design as to indifference. Immigrant trains often ran as extras, going very slowly, and with inadequate accommodations, heat, and water. One observer asserted that better care was taken with cattle shipments. Not infrequently, baggage was misrouted and lost.

By the outbreak of the First World War, millions of immigrants who had seen or experienced adventures such as these had helped to create an America far different from what the founding fathers could have imagined. The ethnic map was sometimes like a checkerboard, showing blocs of one nationality scattered among blocs of other nationalities. Elsewhere it showed a conglomeration of groups of varying size and background, living together in a small area. New York City was an example of both—many nationalities living together in one huge city, yet not really together, for each had its own distinct area of settlement, traces of which remain today, and its own national group organizations.

The areas in which large immigrant groups settled in the 1865–1914 period can be illustrated by the census of 1920. The continuing migration of English and Welsh concentrated heavily in New England but also scattered throughout the nation, including Utah, Michigan, Florida, and the states of the Pacific Coast. The Scots were in much the same areas. The Irish concentrated heavily in New England and the Middle Atlantic states and a few scattered areas; they stayed largely in cities. The Scandinavians settled mostly in the upper Middle West, not so much because of love of cold winters and forests as because of availability of good land at the time they came; they established colonies also in New England, Texas, and the Pacific Northwest. The Dutch who came in the nineteenth century were widely scattered, but had their greatest density in the Middle West, with several close-knit settlements in Michigan, Iowa, and Wisconsin. The Swiss had scattered pockets of heavy concentration, and the French, who really contributed few immigrants, were widely distributed with a relatively greater settlement in the South than most groups. The Germans were also widely dispersed, with heaviest concentrations in the Midwest and Middle Atlantic states. Polish settlement was greatest in the East and the eastern North Central states. The Czechs were similarly located (with significant colonies also in the plains states), as were the Austrians and Hungarians. Yugoslavs were found in Pennsylvania, the Midwest, and, to a lesser extent, in the Far West. Russians settled along the East Coast though some were to be found in the western mountain states. Greeks settled widely, in New England, New York, the Middle West and the Far West, while Italians were to be found mostly in southern New England, the Middle Atlantic regions, in California, and in cities everywhere.

An interesting fact is that the British stocks were generally well dispersed and less likely than other nationalities to settle within the confines of the national group. Partly this may have been because these groups arrived throughout the entire epoch of immigration. But largely it was because of the easier mobility given them by their acquaintance with the English language. Note, too, that again in this period there was little immigration to the Old South. Except for Mexicans in Texas, Cubans in Florida, old French stock in Louisiana, a few other small pockets such as the Germans and Scandinavians in Texas, and the Negroes, the South remained basically of old English stock. The peoples of the new immigration—coming after the closing of the frontier, lacking the capital to buy farms, and generally unskilled and ignorant of the country's language—were unable to go into agriculture, commerce, or the professions. Vast numbers of them became laborers in cities of the northeastern industrial complex, with its voracious market for manpower in its crudest form.

In occupations the trends of the previous period were modified by two factors: the closing of the frontier and the booming industrial economy. Inevitably more and more immigrants became industrial laborers, the newer groups taking the more menial jobs while the groups ahead of them moved into more diverse and better rewarded occupations. The Yugoslavs generally worked in mining or industry, as did the other Slavs, except that those from Dalmatia were fishermen, longshoremen, or sailors as in the old country. Hungarians became laborers and miners but also entered skilled trades, as tailors, or commerce, as operators of small restaurants and stores. Czechs went into industry, also, often in tobacco or clothing. The Italians had a wider experience. In some respects they replaced the Irish, for they became railroad workers and members of construction gangs. Like the Irish, they gradually worked themselves up into the skilled trades and forms of business more advanced than the push carts with which many were forced to begin. Some operated orchards, vineyards, or truck gardens near the cities. Austrians frequently went into personal or domestic service and into industry, becoming tailors, quarrymen, and miners. Immigrants from northern and western Europe were more likely to farm than those from southern and eastern Europe. But as frontier land diminished and farming demanded more and more capital, they, too, tended to come to the cities and take jobs as industrial workers, painters, or decorators or, with the girls especially, as domestic servants. The English and Welsh, for example, were highly concentrated in manufacturing but were also unusually numerous in the professions. Germans were likewise employed mainly in manufacturing, but some were found as saloonkeepers, tailors, and tobacco processors.

The problems and processes of assimilation, with their fascinating variations, are matters that can be studied in almost any community in the country and in innumerable facets—sociological, national, religious, economic, political, historical. The interesting groups include not only the Pilgrims or the French Canadians or the Irish of Boston; not just the immense stream of diversity flowing into and through New York (where as late as 1960 the foreign-born still numbered 20 per cent of the population [1,556,663], and where the children of foreign-born comprised nearly half the people of the city); but the Portuguese in Springfield and Jacksonville, Illinois, and the Dutch in Pella, Iowa, and the Finns in Fitchburg, Massachusetts, or Hancock, Michigan—to say nothing of the people of obvious origins who founded towns like New Edinburg, Arkansas, New Bern, North Carolina, New Sweden, Maine, and 6 different Norways, and countless others. Still, the place names marked only the beginnings. The atmosphere created by national and religious origins might remain strong or weak, yet in the course

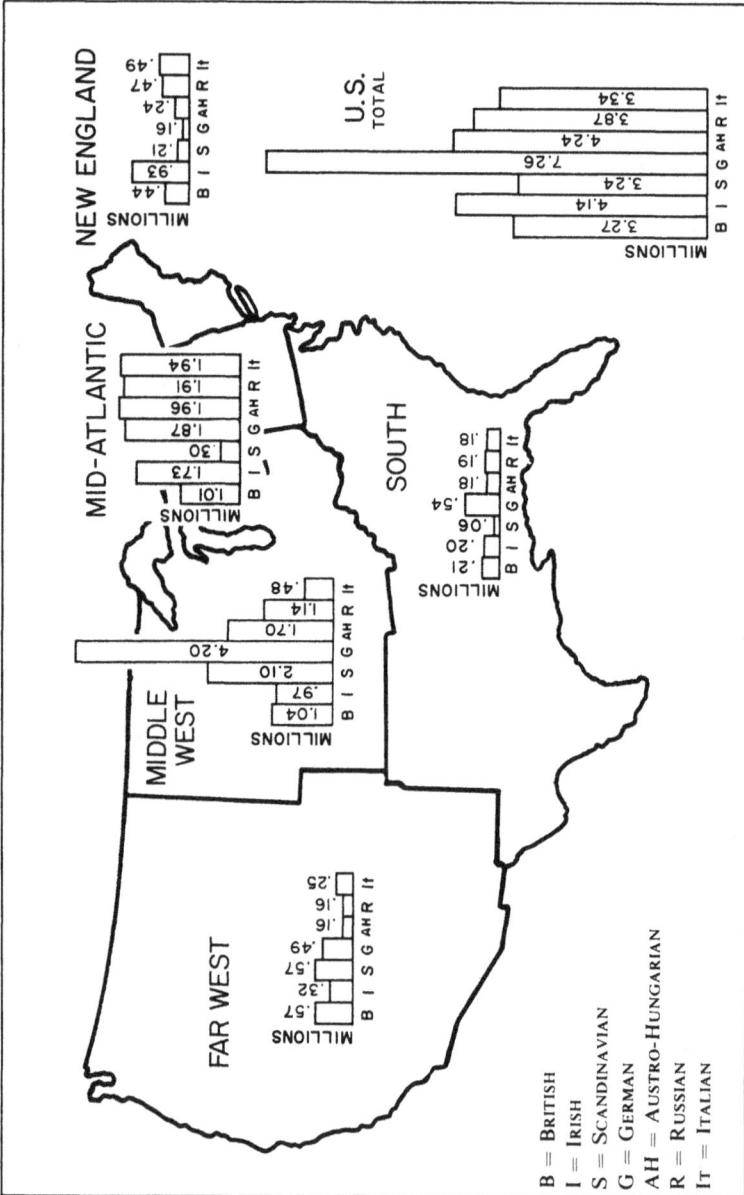

DISTRIBUTION OF FOREIGN STOCK IN THE UNITED STATES ACCORDING
to the Census of 1920

of time the human ingredients usually blended well. The old order faded into increasing revision but did not die, and the infinite variety of America lived on.

Special Cases: Neighbors and Orientals

Although the major movement of American immigration came directly across the Atlantic from Europe, both Latin America and Canada provided side-door entrances and significant original emigration. And immigration from Asia followed different patterns and evidenced special difficulties.

As one historian of immigration, Marcus Lee Hansen, pointed out, the United States and Canada have been interchanging their populations more or less constantly since the flight of the Tories during the American Revolution. The westward movement in each nation was part and parcel of that in the other and caused a constant mingling of peoples. Canadians came south to get Civil War enlistment bounties, or to avoid the impenetrable Laurentian shield which barred internal westward migration, and "Americans" moved north to avoid the Civil War or to pan gold in British Columbia or to raise wheat in Manitoba. They settled each other's prairies and intermingled.

The French-Canadians were an exception. Fortified by language and religion, they tended to remain apart from the main stream of American life. With them the process of assimilation was more like that of other non-English-speaking groups. At one time so many French-Canadians were swarming into New England that they were known as "the Chinese of the Eastern states." They came to take advantage of the economic development of New England; employers liked them for they were reluctant to join unions. In 1930 there were 1,286,000 Canadians in the United States, and in 1950 about 1,000,000, almost one-fourth of them French-Canadian.

The most important of the Latin American nations to contribute to the peopling of the United States has been Mexico. Due to the expansion of the United States into Texas and the territorial gains of the Mexican War, Mexicans there automatically became American citizens. Others came from Mexico to join them, especially after 1900. Between 1909 and 1930 numbers ranging from 11,000 to 89,000 came every year. These were official statistics, but the long desert boundary was easy to cross, and the pressure of economics brought many Mexicans into the United States illegally, not to mention the many who commuted daily to jobs in the United States. Despite the hazard of illegal entry and economic and social discrimination, Mexicans migrated to avoid poverty and misery. By 1930 over 600,000 Mexican-born people lived north of the Rio Grande, and in 1950 the total was still approximately 450,000. The Mexican immigrant at first was primarily an agricultural laborer, because he might earn four times as much north of the Rio Grande as south. Political disorder and religious disturbances were also involved, as were labor recruitment by railroads, agriculture, and factories. When European immigration was curtailed in the 1920's, Mexico became the easiest source of unskilled labor, and Mexican laborers following the harvest northward became a familiar sight. Now they have begun to enter industry, especially in Chicago, Detroit, and Toledo. Even so, the greatest areas of Mexican settlement remain the southwestern states of Texas, Colorado, New Mexico, Arizona, and California. Here too, they have become urbanized, though the city might be their home only during the agricultural "off-season." Mexican assimilation, not simply because of language and racial differences, has been slow and difficult. As one authority puts it: "so many of them are folk people; that is, they have a common body of tradition which is passed on from generation to generation, which determines much of the pattern of their lives." This continuity of Mexican life has been difficult to modify.

Another important Latin American group were the Puerto Ricans, who have been citizens of the United States since 1917. Technically speaking, they were participating in an internal migration. Few had come until the 1920's and even then there were only 70,000 Puerto Ricans on the mainland in 1940. Post-war prosperity and cheap air transport combined to lure them north. The swelling Puerto Rican population of New York, Chicago, and other industrial cities marked this as a significant movement. Their living conditions were inadequate because of their low wages, yet they were better off materially than in Puerto Rico. Handicapped by language, a different cultural background, and sometimes by color, Puerto

Ricans often had to take jobs below their skill levels and work as pressers, floor boys, bus boys, dishwashers, assemblers, or domestics. They found difficult any real integration into the main stream of American life.

The Oriental immigrant also had a special and important place in the history of American immigration. The Chinese were the first from Asia to come to America in significant numbers. Immigration statistics revealed only 88 arrivals from 1820 through 1853, but 13,100 in 1854. Census figures, however, showed 758 people of Chinese birth living in the United States in 1850. Immigration figures showed a total of 41,443 Chinese arrivals through 1860, while census figures had 35,565 Chinese-born residents of the United States that same year. The peak immigration seems to have been in 1882, when official figures showed almost 40,000 arrivals. Some had come to California to participate in the gold rush; their apparent docility and willingness to work assured them a hospitable reception. They became cooks, gardeners, mineworkers and, true to fable, laundrymen. Many were imported especially to work on the transcontinental railroads. Opposition to the Chinese grew, however, on the ground that they were a threat to American labor. Perhaps they were; the Chinese railroad laborer was often paid $30 to $35 per month and most of this he saved. There were also at least two instances in which Chinese laborers were brought East to act as strikebreakers. In California anti-Chinese agitation grew feverish in the 1870's when an Irish immigrant named Dennis Kearney made a series of harangues which led to violence and demands for Chinese exclusion. (It must have been ironic to see him shaking his fist at the Chinese and shouting in a thick Irish brogue, "America fur th' Amerricuns.") As a result local laws discriminated against the Chinese by levying special taxes, imposing regulations on laundries, and by interfering with their customs. In the end federal restrictions were applied (1882), and legal Chinese immigration to the United States ceased for many years.

The next wave of Oriental immigration was that of the Japanese, who began to come in significant numbers about the turn of the century. Before 1886 the largest number to come in any one year was 78 in 1871. By 1891 the figure passed 1,000, and the high point was reached in 1907 with 30,000. Again, census totals indicated more resident Japanese in 1880, for example, than immigration figures showed entered the nation in all previous years. A great population spurt in the Japanese home islands in the last half of the nineteenth century created more mouths than the nation could feed. This plus the recruiting of labor for Hawaiian sugar plantations stimulated emigration; and from Hawaii many made the next step to the mainland. Here they worked as domestics, in mines and lumber camps, and on farms. Unlike the Chinese, they were anxious to become Americanized, and like the Chinese they were regarded as a threat to American labor, which campaigned against them. The eventual result, again, was the exclusion of another stream of immigrants.

The third, and smallest, wave of Oriental immigration came from the Philippine Islands. Though Asians, many Filipinos spoke Spanish, for the islands were a part of the Spanish Empire for over three centuries. Like the Japanese they came first to Hawaii to work the sugar and pineapple plantations. Before 1920 there were few on the mainland, but over 50,000 arrived in the ensuing decade. Because the Philippine Islands were controlled by the United States, the Filipinos were considered nationals and therefore not subject to the quota act. In 1935, however, an independence plan was worked out and a quota established. The Filipinos for the most part did not intend to become permanent residents but came to acquire a stake and then return home. Like the Japanese and Chinese they located primarily on the West Coast and became agricultural laborers or domestics. Though also looked upon as cheap labor, they were not as cheap or docile as Mexicans, Japanese, and Chinese were reputed to be, and they were more willing to join unions. Like other Latin or Oriental groups they have been the victims of extensive job discrimination, and their assimilation has been difficult.

End of an Era

Despite the outbreak of World War I in August, 1914, a total of 1,200,000 immigrants came to the United States that year, slightly more than had come in 1913. But the next four years saw a sharp decline in arrivals, until a low point of 111,000 was reached in

1918. Whereas previously immigration from Canada and Latin America had been a small proportion of the total, during the First World War roughly half of the immigrants were from neighboring countries. Of those who continued to come from Europe during the war, many were from Italy and other countries of southern Europe. The amazing thing is that the European stream continued at all, difficult and indirect as it often had to be. After the war immigration began to pick up again. In 1919, 141,000 immigrants came, but of these 100,000 were from the Western Hemisphere. The largest European contribution was Great Britain's 6,800. In 1920 the figure climbed to 430,000. Over 800,000 arrived in 1921, including 652,000 from Europe, of which the Italians contributed one-third. It seemed that the mass movement had begun again. But then the figure dipped and after 1930, during the years of the Great Depression and World War II, there were never as many as 100,000 new immigrants, and in 1933 and 1943 only 23,000 immigrated to the United States. From 1947 to 1960 the figure varied between 147,000 and 326,000. In 1960 arrivals numbered 265,398, almost half from Europe with Germans making up 29,000. The leading contributor, however, was Canada-Newfoundland with 47,000. Most significant, in the 1930's and the 1940's the outflow from the United States back to Europe frequently surpassed the incoming movement.

Why this change? Why did the teeming masses of the first fourteen years of the twentieth century decline to a comparative handful? Two world wars and a serious depression were major factors. But this is not the whole answer. For a basic change in immigration policy occurred in 1921 which, though modified, remained in effect. Previously the government policy on immigration had been "hands off"—a minimum of control and neither discouragement nor official encouragement of those who wanted to come.

In 1865 a contract labor law was passed, under the encouragement of President Lincoln and the Republican party, to stimulate post-Civil War immigration. It legalized contracts advancing passage funds. But the law was repealed in 1868 under pressure from organized labor, which suspected industry of employing immigrants as strikebreakers and of playing one foreign group off against another. This, union leaders believed, created antagonisms among national groups and thereby diverted attention from the deplorable conditions of their labor. Labor's fears were somewhat unjustified, for industry does not seem to have used the contract labor law to break unions; nevertheless this repeal was an important milestone along the road to immigration restriction.

There had been spotty attempts at immigration restriction. In the colonial period local governments had tried to curb the importation of paupers and convicts, and Pennsylvania had levied a duty on "foreigners and Irish servants, etc." New England tried to prevent the arrival of disfavored religious sects, and in Massachusetts the General Court in 1637 ordered that no stranger could be entertained either privately or publicly for more than three weeks unless permission had been obtained from proper authority. Other colonies tried to discourage the arrival of Quakers or Roman Catholics. In the years after the Revolution only minor state restrictions were imposed, such as those in the 1780's and 1790's prohibiting the importation of convicts. What little action was taken by the federal government was strictly regulatory; thus in 1789 Congress passed naturalization and quarantine laws. The Alien and Sedition Acts of 1798 contained provisions for the deportation of aliens, but these acts were soon repealed. Most immigration laws of the period were of the welfare type. State acts sought registration of new arrivals and prohibition against the coming of paupers, and federal acts quite ineffectively sought to cut the mortality rate of the Atlantic crossing by protecting immigrants from unsanitary conditions and overcrowding.

By the middle of the nineteenth century, however, strong sentiment for immigration restriction had developed, associated with the growth of the nativist movement. Anti-foreign sentiment was not new. Cotton Mather and John Winthrop of colonial Massachusetts disliked the Scotch-Irish, and James Logan as well as Benjamin Franklin inveighed against the German "Palatine boors." Antagonism was also directed against Roman Catholics, who continued to be a primary target of the nativists. Sensational books were published, pointing to dangers of a papist plot and to the moral and political practices of Catholicism. Samuel F. B. Morse, the painter and inventor of the telegraph, took a leading role, publishing such works as *A Foreign Conspiracy against the Liberties of the United*

States and *Confessions of a French Catholic Priest, to Which are Added Warnings to the People of the United States.* Other things aggravated the situation. The Catholic Irish seemed an ill-tempered lot, much given to rowdyism and intemperance, for the noisiest among them gave a reputation to all. Many Protestants rose up in arms when Catholics demanded a share of the state school funds for use in their parochial schools and when Catholics ran a separate ticket in the 1841 elections in New York. Feeling grew intense and violence was all too common.

But the nativist movement was inspired not only by anti-Catholicism. Indeed some nativists were themselves Catholics. One complaint was that immigrants were undercutting the American laborer. Some people objected to the poverty and crime rates of immigrant neighborhoods, and others to their political role, for in some areas they held the balance of power between parties. It took decades to establish the fact that crime rates were related to income and living conditions rather than to national origin. Meantime this anti-foreign sentiment was translated into political action. In 1852 the nativist American party, or "Know-Nothings," advocated the exclusion of foreigners and Catholics from political office and the lengthening of the residence period required for naturalization. For a brief time the party had great success. "America for Americans," was its cry.

America for the Americans! We have had enough of "Young Irelands," "Young Germanys," and "Young Italys." We have had enough of insolent alien threat to suppress out "Puritan Sabbath," and amend our Constitution [a reference to the German forty-eighters]. We have been a patient camel, and borne foreign burden even to the backbreaking pound. But the time is come to right the wrong; the occasion is ripe for reform in whatever we have failed. The politico-religious foe is fully discovered; he must be squarely met, and put down.

In 1856 the party elected eight governors, and in 1857 it had fourteen representatives and five senators. After that it declined steadily and was defunct by 1860. Traditional American ideals triumphed over exclusiveness—for the moment.

Within two decades after the Civil War, nativism again raised its head. Many of the old immigrants were so pro-trade union that they were criticized as much as the anti-union new immigrants were to be later. The Catholic question also emerged once more because of the greatly increased number of Catholics arriving from southern Europe. The American Protective Association, founded in 1887, was both anti-Catholic and anti-immigrant, but it admitted immigrants if they were opposed to the Catholics. The APA gained temporary political influence in the early 1890's, and perhaps its agitation helped to raise standards in both public and parochial schools. But the rifles it purchased never had to be used against an alien priestly plot, and its fear and hate campaign faded out by 1900.

On the West Coast prejudice against the Chinese continued, and the exclusion of 1882 was periodically extended. Soon after the turn of the century, anti-immigrant feelings on the West Coast were directed at the Japanese, and in 1906 the San Francisco school board set up segregated schools for its Japanese, Chinese, and Korean students. Japan protested and President Theodore Roosevelt was greatly embarrassed. He persuaded the school board to rescind its order, but in return he negotiated the "Gentleman's Agreement" by which the Japanese government agreed to stop emigration of laborers to the United States.

Restrictive policies attained a minor success in 1882 with a law excluding all paupers, criminals, and the insane. But nativist and racist attention was turned also to the "new" immigrant. Several violent incidents occurred, including the shooting of Slavic strikers in the Pennsylvania mines and the 1891 lynching of a group of Italian murder suspects in New Orleans. A device was therefore sought which would exclude the southern and eastern European but not the northern and western European, who seemed more intelligent and assimilable (that is, he seemed more like the nativists themselves). To nativist and racist demands were added those of organized labor, which feared cheap foreign competition. Because new immigrants generally were poorly educated, the literacy test was the method hit upon, and after heated debate the American Federation of Labor approved this device. As Senator Henry Cabot Lodge, an early advocate of such a bill, stated in the 1896 debates:

The illiteracy test will bear most heavily on the Italians, Russians, Poles, Hungarians, Greeks, and Asiatics, and very lightly or not at all, upon English-speaking emigrants or Germans, Scandinavians, and French. In other words, the races most affected by the illiteracy test are those whose emigration to this country has begun within the last twenty years and swelled rapidly to enormous proportions, races with which the the English-speaking people have never hitherto assimilated, and who are most alien to the great body of the people of the United States....

The immigrants excluded ... furnish ... a large proportion of the population of the slums ..., who bring least money to the country and who come most quickly upon public or private charity for support.... [and] injure the American wage earner.

The bill was vetoed by President Cleveland, who reminded the restrictionists that although it was said the "quality of recent immigration is undesirable," still "the time is quite within memory when the same thing was said of immigrants who, with their descendants, are now numbered among our best citizens." Other literacy test bills were passed in the Progressive era, but a conservative such as Taft vetoed one in 1913, and the "progressive" Democrat Wilson vetoed one in 1915 and again in 1917, pointing out that each really proposed a penalty for lack of opportunity. In 1917, however, Congress overrode the veto. Exclusionists won a further victory by the almost total prohibition of Asian immigration through the establishment of a "barred zone" which excluded most Asians not already covered by the Chinese Exclusion Acts or the Gentleman's Agreement.

Soon after World War I the increased rate of immigration alarmed a nation which had been stimulated during two years of war into patriotic fervor. Immigrant groups, especially German, were thought to be crawling with spies or beset by foreign communists and anarchists. In the early days of the Red Scare of the 1920's, the real change occurred in American immigration policy. Heretofore there had been no across-the-board restriction. Previous restrictions had been justified on the basis of selecting only the most able and most useful immigrants. But now a policy of numerical restriction was enacted into law. In 1921 the first quota law was established. European immigration for each country was limited to 3 per cent of the number of that nationality present according to the census of 1910, with a yearly maximum of 357,000. In 1924 the maximum was cut in half, the nationality quota was lowered to 2 per cent, and the basis of computation was changed to the census of 1890 (this would favor north and west Europe).

After 1927 the annual maximum was 150,000 (later slightly raised) apportioned by nationality based on the census of 1920. Canadians and Latin Americans were exempt. Again a basic revision of American immigration laws was made in the McCarran-Walter Act of 1952. Passed by the Congress over the veto of President Truman, it codified all previous legislation, kept the quota system and maximum provisions of the 1924 law, but eliminated the absolute exclusion of Asians. Additional provisions designed to prevent admission of subversives and to permit deportation of communists (even if they had become citizens) were controversial but were included in the act.

There were also increased pressures that brought relaxation in America's limitations on immigration. First, Congress voted exceptions for refugee individuals and groups (i.e., the Refugee Relief Act of 1953 which admitted 209,000). Almost 40,000 Hungarians were admitted after their abortive rebellion of 1956, and large-scale exceptions were made for refugees from Castro's Cuba. At last, after vigorous debate, a new immigration act of 1965 provided for the abandonment of the national origins system of the 1920's and all its racist overtones, in favor of more generous treatment of relatives of American citizens and a first-come, first-served policy for 170,000 quota immigrants per year. No single country could send more than 20,000, but non-quota immigrants might add another 100,000 or so altogether.

The impact of restrictions by national origin is difficult to determine. Numbers from some countries were cut drastically, while other countries used but a portion of their quotas. Other factors besides restrictive laws were slowing the flow. Most influential was the economic depression of the early 1930's, when for several years more people left the United States than entered. This remigration, impelled by vast unemployment in the United States, was stimulated by industrial growth in Europe and especially by a German demand for skilled labor in the middle 1930's. The interaction of war, of Europe's need for labor, and of America's legal restriction and depression produced the severe curtailment of immigration to the United States. Cheap land was gone and America could supply most of her demands for labor. A great epoch of transcontinental population movement had come to an end. A new era, with profoundly different social and psychological emphases, was beginning.

Problems of Americanization (except in cities with a large Puerto Rican influx) ceased to be crucial. The numbers of foreign-born declined, and their children were becoming Americans. Czech-Americans married German-Americans, Greek-Americans married old-stock "native" Americans, and most of them came to dislike the hyphen. National group churches had to hold religious services in English. Foreign-language newspapers faded away or became bi-lingual. America letters ceased, until a new prosperity enabled third generation Americans to go back to the old country and search out distant cousins and visit the villages from which grand-parents had come. The children of the era of mass migration had by the mid-twentieth century become rather fully absorbed into the complex of American life, loyalties, and attitudes, and interests were so deeply rooted that they rarely came into question in the hard years of World War II. Even the Japanese-Americans, despite their internment in concentration camps, recognized the United States as their country.

The Wider Perspective of European Emigration

Immense and impressive as is the American saga of immigration, it is well to keep it in perspective, to remind ourselves that other lands also received human wanderers in quantity. Migration was a vast and complex process, and its impact might be almost as important for the country of origin as for the country of destination.

Emigration from Europe was in its seventeenth- and eighteenth-century stages associated with the colonizing enterprise of western European nations. Great Britain was the greatest of the empire builders, using for conquest both a potent navy and a prolific population. From Cape Colony in Africa on the south to Baffin Island on the north, from the Mosquito Coast on the west to New Zealand on the east, the intrepid British explorers, missionaries, merchants, soldiers, and colonists planted the Union Jack. It was a strenuous, often cruel, exciting drama. North America, New Zealand, Australia, and South Africa received hosts of British settlers, not only in the period of deliberate expansion but on into the nineteenth and twentieth centuries.

Other European nations early entered a race for imperialism, but none of them attained the success of the British in providing homes for their own emigrants. The British seemed to have laid their hands on the best of the open spaces of the earth, and the freedom of opportunity allowed in the English possessions was especially appealing to those who wanted to migrate. Thus it was that the American colonies of Spain received few Europeans compared to the great numbers who would come when these nations became independent. The French sent few bona fide settlers anywhere except to Quebec and to their colonies in North Africa. Neither Germany, the Netherlands, nor Italy settled as many people in its colonial empire as it sent to the United States over the last 350 years. In 1914, for instance, less than 24,000 Germans resided in all of Germany's African empire. But emigrants had other choices. While approximately 60 per cent chose the United States, another 40 per cent scattered widely.

The South American countries were popular for several immigrant groups. Brazil, for instance, received large numbers, beginning in the last half of the nineteenth century. Economically attracted by expansion of the coffee industry, most went to the state of São Paulo or to Rio de Janeiro. In the century from 1820 to 1926 at least 4,000,000 immigrants entered Brazil. The largest group were the Italians, with almost 1,500,000. The Portuguese were runners-up, and then came a half million Spaniards, 190,000 Germans, plus Lebanese, Jews, and others. Argentina was also a popular destination for immigrants. Again the largest group were the Italians, who contributed 47 per cent of the total from 1857 to 1926; next were the Spanish, with 32 per cent; and far to the rear came the third-place French, who sent 4 per cent of the 5,741,000 immigrants who entered Argentina in this 70-year span. While this total number does not seem large, in "*intensity* of immigration" (proportion of immigrants to total population) Argentina had for a time a higher immigration rate than the United States. These later waves were, of course, largely of the "new" migration from southern Europe. Canada also had a greater intensity of immigration

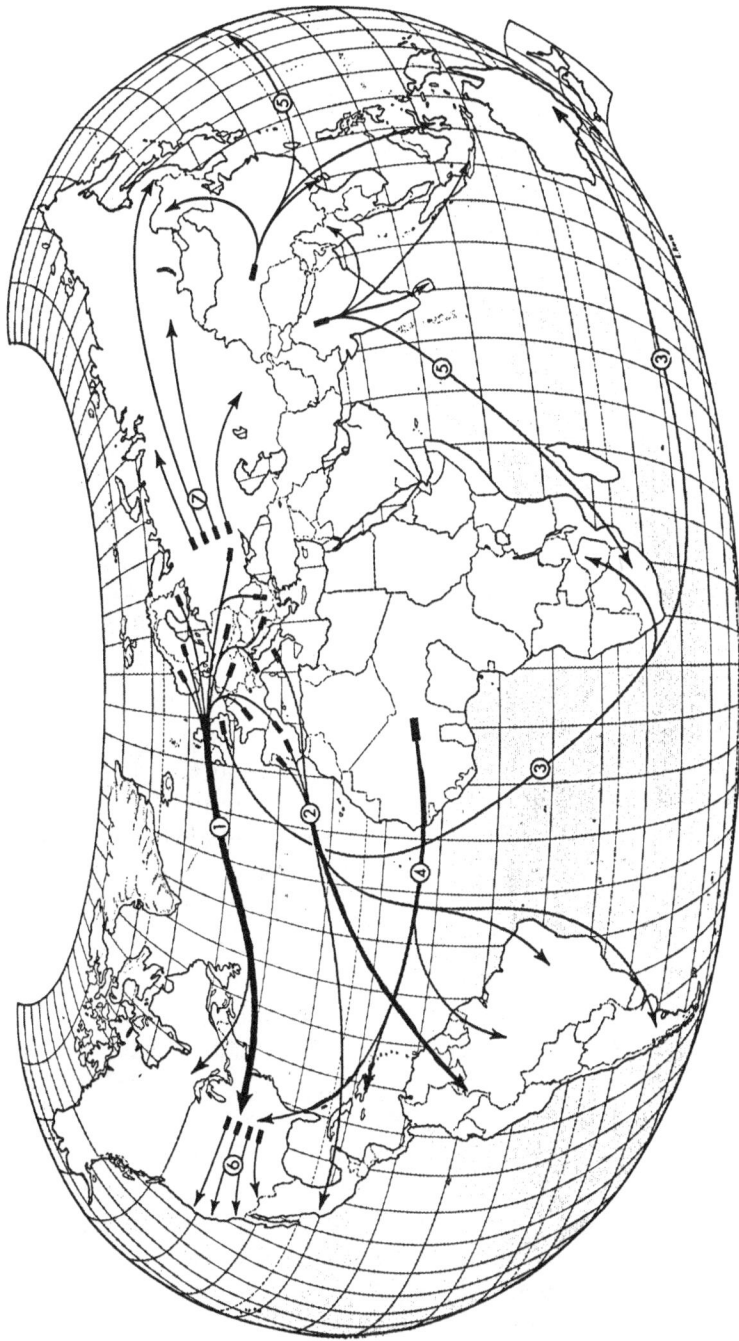

49

than the United States. For the decade 1901–1911, for example, Canadian population jumped from 5,370,000 to 7,200,000. During this time she took in 1,848,000 immigrants, though a high emigration rate left a net immigration of only 980,000.

In addition to European external migration there was much internal migration within Europe. From 1901 to 1905 Italy sent a yearly average of 54,000 persons each to Austria-Hungary, Germany, Switzerland, and France as settlers or as temporary workers. Other Italians went from their sunny but densely-populated homeland to Scandinavia, Russia, Spain, in short, everywhere in Europe. In the years 1876 to 1926, while almost 9,000,000 Italians came to North and South America, another 7,600,000 went to other countries in Europe. This outpouring resulted from a combination of "population explosion" and lack of industrial development.

The vast dislocations caused in Asia and Europe by World War II, the exodus of Jews and other refugees from Europe, the settlement of Israel—these, too, are parts of the saga of human migration.

Especially surprising in the story of European migrations is France. Throughout the nineteenth century French population increased slowly. Between 1871 and 1914 British and German populations grew about one-half, Russian about three-fourths, Italian about one-third, but French less than one-tenth. Between the two world wars France's death rate exceeded the birth rate. Faced with the military and economic implications of such figures, France welcomed immigrants fleeing from population pressures elsewhere in Europe. After the adoption of the quota law by the United States, France became the most important immigrant-receiving country in the world. In 1851 only 1 per cent of the French population were aliens; in 1911 the figure was 3 per cent; by 1931 it had climbed to 7 per cent! In the 'twenties France had a net balance of about 2,000,000 immigrants, of whom more than half came from Poland and Italy. Poland's population density was half again that of France, and its natural increase, 1921–1930, out-numbered that of France eightfold. With small farms and inadequate industry, it was easy for Poland to send thousands to populate a France which had suffered huge war losses from 1914–1918 and which had empty farms and a shortage of labor.

People have always been on the move, and the last two or three centuries were no exception. Chinese left China and settled in the countries of southeast Asia, Japanese went to Formosa and Manchuria, Indians went to Ceylon, Burma, and Malaya, and in the 1830's Boer cattlemen and farmers moved from South Africa deep into the interior to escape restrictions placed upon them by British colonial authorities. Many Europeans went to Africa and Asia: French and Italians settled in Algeria and Tunisia, and, in a migration paralleling our own frontier movement, European Russians penetrated ever deeper into Siberia, while English settled in Australasia. From India thousands went to east and south Africa.

The complexity of the immigration movements becomes more apparent when one considers it as a part of a world trend toward urbanization. In Europe many of the peasants migrated to the towns when displaced by agricultural change which came after the land was divided and "given" to them. Others emigrated overseas, and when they arrived in the new country few had enough resources left to continue their journey to the land. They therefore had to remain in the cities. This was the case most notably with the Irish, and with the southern and eastern European peasants who also lacked capital and who arrived after the cheap western lands were taken. As Frank Thistlethwaite puts it, "by and large, the great migrations after 1890 were from farm to factory, from village to city, whether this meant from Iowa to Chicago, Silesia to Pittsburgh or Piedmont to Buenos Aires."

Thus a rural to urban movement was taking place simultaneously within Europe, within the United States, and between Europe and non-European areas. In 1790, 95 per cent of the population of the United States lived in rural areas. This dropped to 80 per cent in 1860, 60 per cent in 1900, 43 per cent in 1940, and 37 per cent in 1960. The same trend was occurring in Europe. In 1871 one-third of the Germans and one-third of the French lived in towns. By 1914 this was up to two-thirds of the Germans and one-half of the French. In Sweden, less than 10 per cent of the population lived in towns in 1800; the figure was 33 per cent in 1930. In Japan, too, in 1893 only 16 per cent of the population lived in communities of over 10,000 population; in 1925 the figure was 37 per cent. Between 1851 and 1871, for every European who went abroad, 4 or 5 went to Europe's cities.

After World War II, central Europe experienced a convulsive

shift of population as more than 12,000,000 refugees and expellees crowded into West Germany. Not only were they quickly absorbed, but these hardworking immigrants helped to create the "economic miracle." In reinvigorated Germany, and also in Switzerland and Sweden and France, the need for industrial workers grew until by the mid-1960's millions of Turks and Yugoslavs and Italians were streaming northward. Former countries of emigration became countries of immigration. This was a reversal of direction but a continuation of the nineteenth-century pattern that characterized the movement of labor to centers of capital and manufacturing leadership. Simultaneously, a counter movement became obvious. England, for example, received large numbers of unskilled or semi-skilled workers from overseas, but she also sent forth thousands of highly-trained engineers and scientists. This was the "brain drain" that worried statesmen and businessmen alike. Often technicians and managers and teachers, as they migrated to developing countries in Africa and Asia, were accompanied by capital and plans for power plants, factories, and schools. In the nineteenth century, it had been the untrained masses who were mobile; in the twentieth century, increasingly it was the technical experts who moved from country to country, from project to project, wherever the labor supply existed.

Thus the perspective on migration must encompass many different facets of human movement, illustrating the amazing flexibility and adaptability of man to changing circumstances.

The Impact of the Movement on America and on Europe

Wave upon wave, the great outpouring of peoples from Europe through four hundred years had created new nations and cultures. The United States, Canada, Australia, New Zealand, South Africa, all were stamped with European birthmarks. Waves of immigrants have so infiltrated the countries of Latin America that these, too, are more European than Indian. Ripples of the flood have reached into almost every corner of the globe and, in cooperation with forces such as imperialism, commerce, war, and missions, have transformed the planet, have literally "Europeanized" it.

The United States stands, in numbers received and in depth of influence, as the example *par excellence* of a land made by immigration. Since 1600 A.D. somewhere between forty and fifty million immigrants have arrived within America's borders; close to thirty million have stayed. The blending of these peoples and their cultures and their adaptation to American circumstances have created the United States and all its meaning.

The blending itself is hard to describe. It is not a fusion or complete melting together, though it may become so in the course of some thousands of years. Nor is it a continuing separateness of small groups. Special cases like the Amish and the Mennonites are the astonishing exceptions, not the rule. The Scots and the Norwegians and the Lithuanians and the Chinese, and dozens more, celebrate in America their national occasions. But they celebrate also the purely American festivities of the Fourth of July and Thanksgiving. The retention of old loyalties and customs along with the development of new attitudes, affiliations, and practices is one of the fascinating aspects of the migration drama. Each of the new societies has developed its own distinctive character, yet all have retained affinities with the parent cultures. The resultant blending is rather like the tantalizing mixture in a salad bowl where the ingredients remain distinct yet wherein each is flavored by the whole.

The larger of the new cultures, begun by British settlers and infused with many other stocks, kept the English language—with independent modifications which have also enriched the language of England! They have kept more than language, for despite the diversities of national stock these peoples have accepted and clung to other fundamental parts of the British heritage, especially political institutions and ideas, law, and educational patterns. The new communities have offered a chance to choose, and what men have chosen is eloquent testimony to what they preferred. So also was the eager discarding of authoritarianism and artificial distinctions of class. In the new communities men could once more start afresh on the basis not of how they were born, but of what they were able to do. The doors of opportunity swung open; though sometimes they did not swing very wide for the first generation, at least they had no locks, and hope could be sustained.

The tenacity of European culture in motion was evidenced not only in speech and social institutions, but in literature, philosophy, and the arts. It was illustrated perhaps most strikingly in the way people built their homes. For the settlers in America did not adopt the Indian wigwam, nor did those in South Africa copy the native kraal. Where the Europeans went they built as they had built at home—the English built frame houses, the Swedes built log cabins (at first), the Spanish built with balconies and courtyards. And so to this day Durban and Melbourne and Philadelphia look not so different from cities of England and Germany and France. Ways of life that had developed through thousands of years were not to be abandoned. People fled from overcrowding and injustice and hardship, but they had no desire to destroy the good in their past. They wished to preserve their culture, while at the same time they saw the need and the opportunity to refashion it.

A remolding of values and institutions was nevertheless inherent in migration. Sometimes it began early, if indeed the process of Americanization did not begin with the decision to migrate. A certain German immigrant barber, for instance, early in World War II, waved his razor over the head of a native-born, long-time customer and made a memorable speech:

> You think I'm a Nazi, don't you? Well, let me tell you. I fought in the German army in World War I, and I walked through France as a journeyman barber for three years in the 'twenties. I know what it's like over there. I read about America, I studied it. I made up my mind, that's what I want. I learned the Constitution, and I passed the citizenship exam. I chose America, I know what it means. You were just born here, you take it for granted. I bet you I'm a better American than you are!

Assimilation proceeded comparatively easily for such a man. For certain groups such as the English and the Scots, who already knew the language of the country and were in tune with its attitudes, there was usually quick adjustment. For their children the problems could be so few that, as one author put it, "in a sense the British-Americans had no 'second generation.'" For others who immigrated with no knowledge of the language, with no special skill or training, different in religion, appearance, and manners from the majority, the adjustment to American habits could be extremely difficult and might transmit bitterness and complexes to the second and even the third generations. It took a little time for the Irish to learn to laugh at the job advertisements that added the proviso, "No Irish Need Apply." Slum conditions for the newly arrived and ill-paid were often affronts to human dignity. Nevertheless, even out of discrimination and evil conditions there was at least the possibility of improvement of one's lot and of absorption into the larger society.

The contributions made to the new country even by first generation immigrants were beyond man's power of measurement. The sheer human brawn that built railroads and dug canals, that cleared the forests and mined coal, or carried bricks or mixed cement—this was essential to the building of productive power. Some immigrants brought with them higher skills. In one generation alone 25 per cent of the trained graduates of Norwegian technical schools migrated to America, which thus capitalized on education it did not have to pay for! Many of the most notable immigrants were exceptions to the lower middle-class origins of the larger numbers, for even the educated and the well placed sometimes felt frustrated in their native environment or simply saw greater opportunity beckon in America. Albert Einstein was an immigrant, and Fritz Kreisler; so were Louis Agassiz and John J. Audubon, Arturo Toscanini and Serge Koussevitsky. The American press had a long and honorable tradition, but it was enhanced by Joseph Pulitzer and enriched also by the foreign language press which helped to ease the transition of immigrants from one society to another. Now that press is passing from the scene, its purpose fulfilled. It serves as an example of how one generation paves the way for the following, then disappears while leaving its constructive work behind, part of an ongoing contribution.

The Europeanization of America and of the world thus preceded what some have called the Americanization of Europe. The latter term is, of course, a gross exaggeration, and what kernel of truth lies in it is due to many factors besides emigration. Yet, after the term and the idea have been hedged about with caution, it is obvious that both the emigration movement and the great emigrant-receiving country, the United States, have influenced Europe profoundly. This is a subject that has been curiously neglected by European historians and which Americans are only beginning to appreciate and study. At least some of the return effects of emigration are tangible and measurable.

Not only did European descendants in Canada, Australia, South America, and the United States provide food for Europe's increasing millions, they also served as markets for Europe's burgeoning industrial production. Emigration came largely from countries unable to industrialize fast enough to absorb the growing population. The numbers in the labor force were thus held down, which enabled wages to rise for those who stayed. Between 1861 and 1913 agricultural wages in Europe rose for various classes of workers two-and-one-half to four times. Also the productive sons and daughters who had gone to America sent money home in amazing quantity. In Greece, for example, in the early years of the twentieth century such remittances totaled $5,000,000 per year, roughly one-fourth of the country's export income. These funds caused inflation but helped to put the currency on a sound basis, enabled individuals to pay off mortgages, lowered interest rates, and encouraged more people to go to America. Thus by 1909 between one-fifth and one-fourth of the Greek working force was in the United States. To take up the slack, more women entered the work force and thereby changed its composition.

Similar effects were experienced in other nations. In 1907 about 500 million lire were sent to Italy. This improved the foreign exchange value of the lira and was a factor in the reduction of interest rates and in an increase in savings accounts. As with Greece, Italy felt the effect of a smaller supply of agricultural labor, with the result that old men and women were added to the labor force, and wages rose. Sometimes lands were abandoned, and some of the small proprietors who needed extra labor could no longer afford it. Between 1872 and 1900, $96,000,000 went from the United States to the United Kingdom. And there was a definite correlation between the flow of remittances and emigration from Ireland. In Sweden annual remittances from 1906 to 1930 averaged about $8,000,000, the equivalent of one-fourth of the country's balance of payments. (This is a subject that needs careful country-by-country research.)

The physical aspects of a region might also be changed. For remittance money and bequests from overseas could be, and were, used to build homes, churches, and community centers in the old country. Returned immigrants often built new houses, too—more comfortable than those of the "stay-at-homes." The emigrant stimulated the expansion of ports and the building of new ships. The Italian merchant marine never achieved a vigorous state until the emigrant traffic provided the business. And once the emigrants were settled in the new land, the fleet was busy sending Italian products to them. British, German, and Scandinavian lines all thrived on the emigrant business.

Substantial political and social effects of emigration are evident in Sweden, for example. In 1913 a Swedish demographer reported that "to discuss 'Swedish emigration' is the same as to discuss 'Sweden'; there is hardly a single political, social or economic problem in our country which has not been conditioned, directly or indirectly, by the phenomenon of emigration," and a reformer claimed, "We reformers used [emigration] as a vehicle for social legislation." The granting of home loans on easy terms, the development of a frontier in Lappland, the establishment of old age insurance, a state mortgage bank, and universal suffrage, and the adoption of religious freedom came as conscious efforts to make the homeland more attractive to those who might otherwise desire to leave. The military implications of the loss of vast numbers of men of military age were not lost upon those countries which had conscription; accordingly the emigration of such individuals was generally put under some form of control. Because these young males were the most frequent to go, there were important demographic changes in the homelands. Age and sex ratios changed. Rural dislocation was frequent, and new ideas and new money changed old-fashioned ways.

Emigration also had general cultural repercussions, especially in literature. Often the folksong reflected the American experience. The Irishman sang of farewell to Erin:

> Farewell ye green hills and verdant valleys,
> Where I with my sweetheart did often rove,
> Where I vowed her I'd never leave here,
> Whilst walking sweetly through each silent grove.
> But times are changing and crops are failing,
> And causing thousands to go away,
> In deep emotion to cross the ocean,
> To seek their fortunes in America(y).

And Norwegians and Finns and others composed their own emotion-packed salutes.

Language and custom, too, might be changed. Irish speech adopted Americanisms, and one might hear such phrases as, "well, I reckon, as the Yank says." The "American wake" developed, a ceremony of sadness and revelry much like a wake for the dead but occasioned instead by an emigrant's departure to America; for in the early half of the nineteenth century the chance of seeing again the loved one who went to America seemed no greater than if he had gone to the grave. Other influences were stimulated by cultural feedback, that is, communication between the Old and New World. In Greece, for instance, the bachelor returnee was considered especially eligible as a husband, for, influenced by American practice, he was not so likely to demand a dowry when he married. One author concluded that "the marrying Greek-Americans helped to bring economic democracy to the altar." Although the "American," as the returnee might be called, sometimes devoted himself to doing absolutely nothing, others brought a new work-like spirit. It was the Greek-American who often led community efforts for improvement of transportation or health facilities, education, and a more democratic political outlook.

In manifold ways the interchange of peoples and commerce between Europe and America was accompanied by an interchange of ideas, enriching and vitalizing both. Something of the provincialism of thought in the far corners of the European continent was shattered by knowledge of new societies across the sea. The opportunity of an alternative seemed open to everyone, even if he did not take it, and his life was expanded thereby. He became freer. Scientific knowledge grew rapidly as institutions such as the Royal Society in London gathered information from correspondents in the colonies and around the world, and rapidly this new knowledge was organized and published for the use of all peoples. In social ideas the construction of new communities, putting into practice some of the theories evolved by European philosophers, served as a challenge to the tradition-bound communities of Europe and stimulated self-criticism, reform, and revolution.

The interaction of many forces unleashed the emigrant tide, and in its turn migration acted as a creative force in making new societies and transforming old ones. Contrary to the impression given in all too many treatments of immigration, it has not been simply an American manifestation but a phenomenon of world-wide proportions and impact.

NOTES

Because of the impossible bulk of complete documentation, references are given only for quotations and other items that might be difficult to locate. Full bibliographical information, when not supplied here, can be found in the suggested readings.

For statistics on world population and migrations we have relied for the most part on W. S. Woytinsky and E. S. Woytinsky, *World Population and Production* (New York, 1953). Most of the figures on American immigration are taken from *Historical Statistics of the United States.*

The quotation on pp. 11–12 from Franklin is found in F. R. Diffenderffer, *The German Immigration into Pennsylvania*, Part II (Lancaster, 1900), 111. The quotations on p. 18 and p. 19 are from T. C. Blegen, *Norwegian Migration*, 84 and 174; the poem on p. 19 comes from Blegen's *Norwegian Emigrant Songs and Ballads* (Minneapolis, 1936), 120; and two of those on p. 21 are from Blegen's *Land of Their Choice*, 55 and 184–186. The quotation on p. 43 is from Edith Abbott, *Historical Aspects*, 793; that on pp. 44–45 from Abbott's *Immigration: Select Documents*, 193–194. The quotations on pp. 28 and 30 are from W. I. Thomas and F. Znaniecki, *Polish Peasant in Europe and America*, Vol. II of the 1918 edition, 110, 249–250, 220. On p. 57 the first quotation is as given in English from Thistlethwaite's article cited below, 37; the second is cited in F. D. Scott, "The Study of the Effects of Emigration," *Scandinavian Economic History Review* (VIII [1960], 161–174), 170; and the Irish verse is from Arnold Schrier, *Ireland and the American Emigration*, 95.

SUGGESTIONS FOR FURTHER READING

Migrations in general are analyzed in a small volume by the Finnish scholar Ragnar Numelin, *The Wandering Spirit, A Study of Human Migration* (London, 1937), emphasizing geographic and economic impulses. Another study concerned with the purposeful movement of large groups of people from ancient times on is H. C. Morris, *History of Colonization*, 2 vols. (New York, 1900). A one-volume survey, both historical and sociological in nature, is Maurice R. Davie, *World Immigration, With Special Reference to the United States* (New York, 1936). More detailed is the treatment by Walter F. Willcox, ed., *International Migrations*, 2 vols. (New York, 1929–31); volume one is primarily statistical, volume two is interpretative. Comparable in scope is Donald R. Taft, *Human Migration, A Study of International Movements* (New York, 1936), and the revision by Taft and Richard Robbins, *International Migrations, the Immigrant in the Modern World* (New York, 1955), which concentrates on the period since 1918. The authors see migration "as one of many threads interwoven in a changing pattern of social relations among men." See also Brinley Thomas, ed., *Economics of International Migrations* (London, 1958).

A stimulating general treatment is Frank Thistlethwaite's "Migration from Europe Overseas in the Nineteenth and Twentieth Centuries," reprinted along with other essays in Herbert Moller, ed., *Population Movements in Modern European History* (New York, 1964). Thistlethwaite reminds us that American immigration has tended to be overemphasized and that there has been all too little research regarding the emigration from Europe; he calls attention to the importance of the impact of migration on the sending as well as receiving countries. Mack Walker has recently published a lively and thoughtful essay focused on one sending country: *Germany and the Emigration 1816-1885* (Cambridge, Mass., 1964). George Pierson writes delightfully on American mobility in "The M-Factor in American History," *The American Quarterly* (Summer 1962, Supplement), 275-289; in "A Restless Temper . . . ," *American Historical Review*, LXIX (July, 1964), 969-989; and in other articles.

Unfortunately, most of the studies that have even begun to appraise the effect of the outbound movement on the home countries are still in scattered articles, rather than in books. Among the notable exceptions are Arnold Schrier, *Ireland and the American Emigration 1850-1900* (Minneapolis, 1958), which discusses American influences which "filtered back to Ireland via the emigrant stream"; a similar study by Theodore Saloutos, *They Remember America: The Story of the Repatriated Greek-Americans* (Berkeley and Los Angeles, 1956); and one of the earliest cross-cultural studies of all, that by William I. Thomas and Florian Znaniecki, *The Polish Peasant in Europe and America,* 2 vols. (2nd ed., New York, 1927). The latter contains much documentary source material. Other notable special collections are by Theodore C. Blegen, ed., *Land of Their Choice, The Immigrants Write Home* (Minneapolis, 1955), containing letters of Norwegian immigrants which helped to spur the "American fever," and Alan Conway, ed., *The Welsh in America. Letters From the Immigrants* (Minneapolis, 1961). A specific and different kind of study of the social effects of emigration is Franklin D. Scott, "Sweden's Constructive Opposition to Emigration," *Journal of Modern History*, XXXVII (September, 1965), 307-335. On the still broader problems of cultural interchange two useful studies are Michael Kraus, *The Atlantic Civilization: Eighteenth Century Origins* (Ithaca, 1949), and Walter P. Webb, *The Great Frontier* (Boston, 1952). William H. McNeill's *Rise of the West* (Chicago, 1963) is imbued throughout with emphasis on migration and diffusion.

For the specifically American side of the immigration story any one of several volumes can serve as introduction: both George M. Stephenson, *A History of American Immigration 1821-1924* (Boston, 1926), and Carl Wittke, *We Who Built America, The Saga of the Immigrant* (New York, 1939), emphasize the role of the various nationality groups in their adaptation to and influence on American culture. Marcus L. Hansen, in *The Atlantic Migration, 1607-1860. A History of the Continuing Settlement of the United States* (Cambridge, Mass., 1940), began a scholarly treatment of American immigration, but due to his untimely death the series was never completed. A recent readable survey is Maldwyn A. Jones, *American Immigration* (Chicago, 1960), which de-emphasizes the difference between the old and the new immigration and takes as its basic theme "how inheritance and environment interacted." The papers presented by a group of specialists at a conference in honor of Dean Blegen are edited by H. S. Commager under the title *Immigration and American History* (Minneapolis, 1961). Other useful collections of essays are Fritiof Ander, ed., *In the Trek of the Immigrants* (Rock Island, 1964) and Michael Kraus, ed., *The American Mosaic* (Princeton, 1966). See also John F. Kennedy, *A Nation of Immigrants* (New York, 1964). Provocative interpretations of migration and cultural transfer are found in Daniel J. Boorstin, *The Americans,* 2 vols. (New York, 1958, 1965), and Howard Mumford Jones, *O, Strange New World* (New York, 1964).

General treatments of immigration in the colonial period can be found in any good text on American colonial history, such as Oliver P. Chitwood, *A History of Colonial America* (3rd ed., New York, 1961), and Curtis P. Nettels, *The Roots of American Civilization, A History of American Colonial Life* (New York, 1938). The special subject of the indentured servant is exhaustively treated in Abbot E. Smith, *Colonists in Bondage, White Servitude and Convict Labor in America 1607-1776* (Chapel Hill, 1947). On the slave trade, Ulrich Bonnell

Phillips, *American Negro Slavery* . . . (Gloucester, Mass., 1959), and John Hope Franklin, *From Slavery to Freedom; a History of American Negroes* (2nd ed., New York, 1956), have good chapters. See also Lerone Bennett, *Before the Mayflower; a History of the Negro in America 1619–1962* (Chicago, 1963). A unique treatment of the role of women in the building of the early frontier is Eugenie Andruss Leonard, *The Dear-Bought Heritage* (Philadelphia, 1965). Two early nineteenth-century accounts of both the European and American scene are reproduced in R. H. Billigmeier and F. A. Picard, *The Old Land and the New: The Journals of Two Swiss Families in America in the 1820's* (Minneapolis, 1965).

For American history after independence, studies of national immigrant groups become important despite the fact that many of them eulogize overmuch the glorious contributions of the author's ancestors. One of the earliest of these studies is Albert B. Faust, *The German Element in the United States, With Special Reference to its Political, Moral, Social and Educational Influence*, 2 vols. (New York, 1927). Useful studies of the Scots and Scotch-Irish are Henry Jones Ford, *The Scotch-Irish in America* (Princeton, 1915), Ian C. C. Graham, *Colonists from Scotland: Emigration to North America, 1707–1783* (Ithaca, 1956), and Wayland F. Dunaway, *The Scotch-Irish of Colonial Pennsylvania* (Chapel Hill, 1944). The finest example of historical scholarship in this group of studies is Theodore C. Blegen, *Norwegian Migration to America*, 2 vols. (Northfield, Minn., 1931–40); Dean Blegen is also indirectly responsible for forty-odd volumes of publications by the Norwegian American Historical Society. Other useful works treating the Northern peoples include Florence Edith Janson, *The Background of Swedish Immigration, 1840–1930* (Chicago, 1931), and George M. Stephenson, *The Religious Aspects of Swedish Immigration* (Minneapolis, 1932). For the Dutch there is the thorough treatment by Henry S. Lucas, *Netherlanders in America, Dutch Immigration to the United States and Canada, 1789–1950* (Ann Arbor, 1955), which emphasizes the religious motivation in contrast to the other studies, most of which give pre-eminence to the economic. On the role of the Irish is the good study by Carl Wittke, *The Irish in America* (Baton Rouge, 1956). For the English, who blended quickly and unobtrusively into America life, there are comparatively few special studies, but one valuable exception is Rowland T. Berthoff, *British Immigrants in Industrial America, 1790–1950* (Cambridge, Mass., 1953), which points out the importance of the technical skills and experience of English workmen. Robert F. Foerster, *The Italian Emigration of Our Times* (Cambridge, 1919), treats Italian migration to other countries of Europe, North Africa, and South America, as well as to the United States, and though early is objective in approach. A case study of assimilation is offered in Irvin L. Child, *Italian or American? The Second Generation in Conflict* (New Haven, 1943). Theodore Saloutos, *The Greeks in the United States* (Cambridge, 1964), emphasizes the dual affiliations with old country and new. Joseph A. Wytrwal, *America's Polish Heritage. A Social History of the Poles in America* (Detroit, 1961), is another good national-group study, and the blending of many groups is well portrayed in Rudolph J. Vecoli's *The People of New Jersey* (Princeton, 1965).

For accounts of population movements concerning our nearest neighbors, there are the studies by Marcus Lee Hansen, *The Mingling of the Canadian and American Peoples* (New Haven, 1940), and Manuel Gamio, *Mexican Immigration to the United States. A Study of Human Migration and Adjustment* (Chicago, 1930). Mr. Gamio also has a volume, *The Mexican Immigrant, His Life Story* (Chicago, 1931), containing autobiographical sketches of seventy-six Mexican immigrants. The large Puerto Rican influx is studied by C. Wright Mills, Clarence Senior, and Rose Kohn Goldsen, *The Puerto Rican Journey, New York's Newest Migrants* (New York, 1950), and by Oscar Handlin, *The Newcomers* (Cambridge, 1959). Puerto Ricans, Mexicans, and Filipinos are discussed in the brief survey by John H. Burma, *Spanish-Speaking Groups in the United States* (Durham, N. C., 1954).

Useful studies of Oriental immigration are rare. The best for the Chinese is Mary Roberts

Coolidge, *Chinese Immigration* (New York, 1909), which is concerned almost entirely with the American experience, the movement for restriction, and the process of assimilation. There are two up-to-date studies: S. W. Kung, *Chinese in American Life* (Seattle, 1962), and Gunther Barth, *Bitter Struggle. A History of the Chinese in the United States, 1850–1890* (Cambridge, 1964). For the Japanese see Yamato Ichihashi, *Japanese in the United States. A Critical Study of the Problems of the Japanese Immigrants and Their Children* (Stanford, Calif., 1932). For a glimpse of problems outside the United States see A. T. Yarwood, *Asian Migration to Australia . . . 1896–1923* (Melbourne, 1964).

General document collections of value are the two volumes by Edith Abbott, ed., *Historical Aspects of the Immigration Problem. Select Documents* (Chicago, 1926), and *Immigration, Select Documents and Case Records* (Chicago, 1924), and also the brief but well selected documents in Oscar Handlin, ed., *Immigration as a Factor in American History* (Englewood Cliffs, N. J., 1959). For governmental documents the most valuable collection is probably *Reports of the Immigration Commission*, 61 Cong., 3 Sess. (Washington, 1911), in 41 volumes, the report of the Dillingham Commission, which covers conditions in Europe, occupations and working conditions of immigrants, crime, legislation, and many other topics. One must be forewarned that it has an anti-new immigrant bias. All the volumes of the United States census are valuable. For statistical summaries see *The Statistical History of the United States from Colonial Times to the Present* (Stamford, Conn., 1965), and E. P. Hutchinson, *Immigrants and their Children, 1850–1950* (New York, 1956).

The galaxy of special topics related to immigration present manifold possibilities for reading and study. Edwin C. Guillet, *The Great Migration. The Atlantic Crossing by Sailing-Ship Since 1770* (New York, 1937), is a dramatic description of conditions in ports at both ends of the immigrant journey and aboard ship. Colonization activities of the railroads are examined in Paul W. Gates, *The Illinois Central Railroad and Its Colonization Work* (Cambridge, 1934), and in Richard C. Overton, *Burlington West. A Colonization History of the Burlington Railroad* (Cambridge, 1941). The problems of immigrants in American cities and the impact of immigrants upon politics and other aspects of life therein are treated in such books as Oscar Handlin, *Boston's Immigrants, A Study in Acculturation* (rev. ed., Cambridge, 1959), Robert Ernst, *Immigrant Life in New York City 1825–1863* (New York, 1949), Moses Rischin, *The Promised City. New York's Jews. 1870–1914* (Cambridge, 1962), and Nathan Glazer and Patrick Moynihan, *Beyond the Melting Pot* (Cambridge, 1964), which deals with five migrant groups in New York City.

The problem of restrictive legislation is comprehensively handled in Roy L. Garis, *Immigration Restriction; A Study of the Opposition to and Regulation of Immigration into the United States* (New York, 1927), wherein the author argues that "legislation of today is not a thing of the moment but the product of almost two hundred years of study and thought by the American people." See also John Higham, *Strangers in the Land. Patterns of American Nativism, 1860–1925* (New Brunswick, 1955), and Marion T. Bennett, *American Immigration Policies* (Washington, D. C., 1963). On the law of 1965, see Oscar Handlin, "Party of One—Americanizing our Immigration Laws," *Holiday*, XXXIX (January, 1966), 8–13. Somewhat differing views on this subject are taken up in William S. Bernard, ed., *American Immigration Policy—A Reappraisal* (New York, 1950), and Robert A. Divine, *American Immigration Policy, 1924–1952* (New Haven, 1957).

In many of the books mentioned the emphasis is on the causes, impact, and statistics rather than upon the personal equation which was of all-encompassing importance for the individual immigrant and his family. Oscar Handlin in *The Uprooted. The Epic Story of the Great Migrations That Made the American People* (Boston, 1952), takes as his theme, "emigration is the central experience of a great many human beings," and tells the poignant story of those who fled from hardship and of the disillusionment which so many of them met in the slums and the back-breaking jobs in the New World. After reading this, one should see also the reaction by Rudolph Vecoli, "Contadini in Chicago: A Critique of *The Uprooted*," *Journal of American History*, LI (December, 1964), 404–417. Personal memoirs are innumerable, one recent and beautifully-written example being Paul Knaplund, *Moorings Old and New* (Madison, 1963). Writers of fiction have sometimes caught the profound drama of human transplanting. Among the most successful are Ole E. Rolvaag, *Giants in the Earth; A Saga of the Prairie* (New York, 1927), which deals with the hard life of Norwegian immigrants in South Dakota, and Vilhelm Moberg in his impressive trilogy: *The Emigrants* (New York, 1951), *Unto a Good Land* (New York, 1954), and *The Last Letter Home* (New York, 1962), which is the long saga of a particular group of Swedish immigrants who settled in Minnesota.

Books have absorbed and portrayed only part of the literature available. Various periodicals and reviews, and particularly those of national group societies, have excellent material to offer. Among these might be mentioned as examples the *German-American Review*, *Norwegian-American Studies*, and the *Swedish Pioneer Historical Quarterly*. *International Migration*, published in a trilingual edition in The Hague, is a continuation of the *REMP Bulletin* and *Migration* of the Intergovernmental Committee for European Migration; it emphasizes current problems of refugee movements.

To supplement this selective sample of books in the vast area of migration, the reader will find useful the extensive bibliography in *A Report on World Population Migrations, as Related to the United States of America* (Washington, 1956), which contains hundreds of entries for American immigration, and immigration in general, and also discusses specific problems of migration. Literature is developing on African migration, too considerable to be surveyed here, but examples worth citing are Hilda Kuper, ed., *Urbanization and Migration in West Africa* (Los Angeles, 1965), and the bibliography by Ruth Simms, *Urbanization in West Africa* (Evanston, 1965). Current publications are listed in *Immigration Research Digest* (Population Studies Center, Department of Sociology, University of Pennsylvania, Philadelphia), in *Population Index*, quarterly (Princeton Office of Population Research) and in *International Migration Review* (New York and Rome). An extensive though out-of-date bibliography is provided by Dorothy S. Thomas, *et al.*, *Research Memorandum on Migration Differentials* (New York, 1938).

Opportunities for the local study of immigration exist in almost every community in the United States, and in many cases it is not too late still to gather firsthand material, both oral and written, from some of those who took part in the "great migration" itself. A recent article suggesting new possibilities is Timothy L. Smith's "New Approaches to the History of Immigration in Twentieth-Century America," *American Historical Review*, LXXI (July, 1966), 1265–1279. In many communities recent refugees can tell why they had to flee, why they came to America. In other communities special national groups still retain their old customs, their special religious beliefs, even sometimes special forms of dress. Many of the colleges founded to preserve foreign culture and blend it with the best in America have collections of books and manuscripts which need to be studied and interpreted before they disintegrate. Church records and old newspapers contain revealing clues to the past and to the process by which Europeans have become Americans. Immigration is a "live" historical subject.

Of direct use to high school teachers and students are the localized history pamphlets on nationality groups being published in 1967 by Teachers College Press, Columbia University, under the editorship of Clifford L. Lord. First to appear are Einar Haugen, *The Norwegians in America*, Carl Wittke, *The Germans in America*, and Theodore Saloutos, *The Greeks in America*.

www.ingramcontent.com/pod-product-compliance
Lightning Source LLC
Chambersburg PA
CBHW022131280326
41933CB00007B/638